PERFECT PICNICS

PERFECT PICNICS

CATHERINE REDINGTON

ILLUSTRATIONS BY
ANTONIA ENTHOVEN

NEW
ORCHARD

CONTENTS

INTRODUCTION

Planning a perfect picnic is, in my opinion, as much an art as planning a luncheon or dinner party. The requirements are very similar. At home, you want your guests to enjoy the occasion, so you plan ahead, arranging the setting with lighting and flowers. Table linen is the best you have and the room is arranged to establish a welcoming ambience.

You go through your recipes, choosing more sumptuous dishes than you would for an every-day occasion, suited to your guests and the occasion, and select wines to complement the menu.

Everything is planned down to the last detail so that the party goes smoothly and without a hitch. And, at the end, you congratulate yourself on a successful party.

Admittedly, in planning a perfect picnic, you cannot plan good weather also, and in the best-laid plans, nature has a way of getting involved with unexpected winds blowing up from nowhere, or any army of ants deciding to march through the middle of your site. But, assuming that you've taken the precautions of checking weather forecasts and of choosing the venue fairly carefully, a picnic can be as enjoyable, and as glamorous an occasion as any party held in indoor surroundings.

For most people, the ideal picnic conjures up an image of a snowy cloth spread under trees with sunlight glinting through the leaves and cool water nearby. Conversation is lazy and relaxed, the food light, appetizing and delicious and a glass of wine helps it down. This is my idea of an ideal picnic also but there are other times of the year, and occasions, that can be just as enjoyable as the perfect summer's afternoon.

The long, summer evenings are, of course, wonderful for picnic entertaining, whether in your own garden or at a special social event such as an open air concert or the theatre. Sports occasions, race meetings, regattas are also an opportunity for inviting friends to share a special picnic lunch or tea.

Other seasons offer their own particular pleasures: an afternoon's walk in autumn could culminate in a delicious, old-fashioned tea or an excursion on a crisp winter's day might be an opportunity to invite friends to a winter sporting event and you make the occasion special with hot mulled drinks, warming soups or casseroles, and flaky parcels of meat or chicken, easy to eat and delicious. The early days of spring encourage us to think of venturing on the first picnics of the year, and of course, family parties, especially where there are children, are perfect times for outdoor entertaining.

The perfect picnic, to me, has three things: first, the food has to be good and varied – as good as you would eat at home, beautifully presented and with all the right accompaniments and garnishes. That is what this book is about – good, if sometimes unusual, picnic dishes for every kind of occasion.

Next, I see no reason why one shouldn't eat from proper plates with knives, forks, spoons and so on, and drink from cups and glasses. For a special occasion, when the bulk of the picnic is no problem, I would take real chinaware and glasses – but there are excellent ranges of attractive plasticware available – and non-breakable 'glasses' also. I like to use a crisply laundered tablecloth and real table napkins, but for a rambling picnic, paper serviettes will do, but make sure they are large and thick. Finally, for the perfect picnic, hot food should be hot, and cold food really cold, and you will achieve this happy state with insulated bags and boxes.

Of course, you will not always go to all this trouble for a picnic. There will always be times when you say 'isn't it a lovely day – let's go out and take a picnic' and on these occasions, you will choose some delicious foods from your store cupboard and freezer, pre-planned and pre-cooked for just such a time, and it will still turn out to be a perfect picnic.

AT THE WATER'S EDGE

The shore of a lake, or a beach by the sea are tempting places to picnic: the water provides an attractive backdrop and a marvellous playground for the energetic. With the help of watertight bags, rigid containers and ice packs, waterside picnics can be dazzlingly elegant.

Even the keenest swimmer will be tempted out of the water by the thought of an Avocado Swirl or Mushroom Terrine. Serve these as appetizers with brown bread or melba toast, or as a main dish with salads. The Poached Salmon and Orange Glazed Gammon both make fine centrepieces for the main course. A couple of glasses of refreshing Summer Sparkler should ensure that the afternoon is taken at a pleasantly leisurely pace.

FILO ONION TARTS

APPETIZER   MAKES 15

10 sheets filo pastry (strudel leaves), thawed if frozen
50g/2oz butter, melted
FILLING
1 large onion, peeled and thinly sliced
25g/1oz butter
150ml/¼ pint single cream
1 egg, beaten
freshly-ground black pepper
2 × 15ml spoons/2 tablespoons Parmesan,
freshly-grated
1 × 15ml spoon/1 tablespoon pinenuts

Lay a sheet of filo pastry on the work surface. Brush it well with melted butter and lay another piece of pastry on top. Continue buttering and layering until you have a stack of 10 buttered sheets. Cut the pastry into 15 squares (5 × 3). Working quickly before the butter sets, ease each square into a bun tin to make a pastry cup.

To make the filling, fry the onion in the butter for 4 minutes until softened but not coloured. Divide the onion equally between the pastry cups.

Blend the cream, egg and plenty of freshly-ground black pepper until smooth. Pour over the onion in the cups. Sprinkle each with Parmesan and a few pinenuts. Bake at 200°C/400°F/Gas 6 for 10 to 15 minutes until set and golden.

Cool completely before packing.

AVOCADO SWIRL

APPETIZER   SERVES 8-10

40g/1½oz butter
25g/1oz plain flour
1 × 5ml spoon/1 teaspoon mustard powder
150ml/¼ pint milk
3 eggs, separated
FILLING
1 avocado, peeled and stoned
2 × 5ml spoons/2 teaspoons lemon juice
1 × 5ml spoon/1 teaspoon paprika pepper
50g/2oz curd cheese
50g/2oz cream cheese, softened
1 × 15ml spoon/1 tablespoon Parmesan cheese,
freshly grated
2 × 15ml spoons/2 tablespoons thick mayonnaise
freshly-ground white pepper
GARNISH
paprika pepper

Melt the butter in a small pan and stir in the flour and mustard. Cook gently without colouring for 2 minutes. Gradually add the milk and beat well after each addition until a smooth, thick sauce is formed. Remove from the heat and allow to cool for 2 minutes. Beat in the egg yolks.

Whisk the egg whites stiffly in a clean bowl. Beat 1 × 15ml spoon/1 tablespoon of egg white into the sauce mixture. Fold in the remaining egg white. Spread the mixture evenly into a greased and lined 23 by 30cm/9 by 12inch swiss roll tin.

Bake at 190°C/375°F/Gas 5 for 15 to 20 minutes. The roulade will be risen and golden when ready. Turn out onto greaseproof paper and roll up with the paper. Allow to cool.

To make the filling, mash together all the ingredients until smooth. Season to taste with freshly-ground white pepper. Unroll the roulade, remove the paper and spread generously with the filling. Roll it up again and chill for at least 1 hour before transporting.

Pack in a rigid container and cut into slices just before serving.

SERVING SUGGESTION   Slices of Avocado Swirl can be eaten with thinly-cut brown bread and butter or, for a more substantial meal, served with a rice salad.

MUSHROOM TERRINE

APPETIZER   SERVES 6-8

1 small onion, finely chopped
2 cloves garlic, peeled and crushed
175g/6oz butter
450g/1 lb mushrooms, roughly chopped
150ml/¼ pint red wine
2 bay leaves
15g/½oz aspic powder
300ml/½ pint hot white stock
175g/6oz cream cheese
2 × 15ml spoons/2 tablespoons mayonnaise
freshly-ground black pepper
dash Worcestershire sauce
few drops Tabasco sauce
GARNISH
sliced mushrooms

Fry the onion and garlic in the butter for 5 minutes until softened. Add the mushrooms, wine and bay leaves. Bring the mixture to the boil and simmer until the liquid is reduced by half. Remove the bay leaves. Dissolve the aspic powder in the hot stock and add to the mushrooms. Pour the contents of the saucepan into a food processor or blender and work to a purée. Allow to cool slightly then blend in the cream cheese and mayonnaise. Season with freshly-ground black pepper and a dash of Worcestershire sauce and Tabasco sauce. Pour the mixture into a polythene film-lined loaf tin. Chill until completely set.

Transport the terrine in the loaf tin. Turn out the terrine at the picnic and peel away the polythene film.

SERVING SUGGESTION   Garnish with raw mushroom slices and serve with crackers or melba toast as an appetizer or as a choice of main dish in a meal of several dishes.

POACHED SALMON

MAIN DISH   SERVES 6-8

2.7kg/6lb piece of salmon or whole sea trout, cleaned
small bunch of parsley, chopped
150ml/¼ pint dry white wine
50g/2oz unsalted butter, flaked
½ lemon, sliced
15g/½oz aspic powder
freshly-ground white pepper
GARNISH
1 lemon, sliced
¼ cucumber, sliced
watercress

Place the fish in the centre of a large piece of foil. Sprinkle over the parsley and flakes of butter. Pour over the wine. Arrange the lemon slices along the fish. Season with freshly-ground white pepper. Bring the edges of the foil together and make a neatly sealed parcel. Place on a baking sheet and bake at 180°C/350°F/Gas 4 for 30 minutes or until the fish is opaque when the flesh is parted with a knife tip. Remove from the baking sheet but leave in the foil until cold.

Unwrap the fish and discard the parsley and lemon. Strain the cooking liquor and reserve. Carefully peel the skin away from the flesh and smooth away any dark flesh. Leave the head and tail in position if you are using a whole fish. Lay the fish in a spacious, shallow transportable container.

Make up the fish liquor to 300ml/½ pint with boiling water. Dissolve the aspic powder in the water, heating it a little more to completely dissolve the aspic if necessary. Cool the aspic jelly until it thickens a little, then spoon it evenly over the fish, retaining some.

Garnish the fish with slices of lemon and cucumber and spoon a little more aspic over the garnish to keep it fresh. Surround the fish with watercress and chill until required.

For a picnic with several guests, transport the fish whole in the container. Alternatively, cut individual portions and arrange them on plates, covering the fish with polythene film.

ORANGE GLAZED GAMMON

MAIN DISH   SERVES 6-8

1.8kg/4 lb gammon joint
600ml/1 pint medium dry cider
150ml/¼ pint orange juice
whole cloves
GLAZE
1 × 15ml spoon/1 tablespoon clear honey
2 oranges, finely grated rind only
2 × 15ml spoons/2 tablespoons demerara sugar
2 × 15ml spoons/2 tablespoons wholegrain mustard

Place the gammon joint in a large pan and cover with cold water. Bring the water to the boil. Remove from the heat and drain the gammon. Pour in the cider and orange juice and just enough fresh water to cover the joint. Bring to the boil and then reduce the heat to a simmer. Cover the pan and cook for 1 hour and 5 minutes. Drain the joint and leave until cool enough to handle. Strip off the rind using a small sharp knife, to leave the fat exposed. Score the fat into diamonds and press a clove into the fat at each intersection. Place the gammon in a lightly oiled roasting tin.

Mix together the ingredients for the glaze and spread the mixture evenly over the fat. Bake at 200°C/400°F/Gas 6 for 35 minutes. Allow to cool completely.

To transport, wrap whole in polythene film and then foil. Carve the gammon at the picnic. Alternatively, carve at home and wrap individual portions.

SERVING SUGGESTION Serve gammon slices with potato salad or green salad.

ROAST PISTACHIO CHICKEN

MAIN DISH   SERVES 4-6

1 bunch spring onions, trimmed and chopped
25g/1 oz butter
100g/4 oz fresh breadcrumbs
2 × 15ml spoons/2 tablespoons fresh parsley, chopped
40g/1½ oz shelled pistachio nuts, coarsely chopped
75g/3 oz cream cheese
1 egg, beaten
450ml/¾ pint chicken stock
1.6kg/3½ lb roasting chicken
25g/1 oz butter, melted
freshly-ground black pepper

Fry the onion in the butter, until softened. Stir in the breadcrumbs, parsley, nuts, cream cheese and beaten egg. Season with freshly-ground black pepper. Knead with the hands until smooth. Rinse the chicken inside and out and wipe dry with absorbent kitchen paper. Place the chicken with the neck facing you. Insert your fingers between the flesh and breast skin. Carefully loosen the skin from the breast and thighs. Spread the stuffing evenly under the skin. Reshape the bird with your hands. Place the chicken on a trivet in a roasting tin. Brush all over with melted butter and pour the stock into the tin. Season with black pepper and cover with foil. Roast at 190°C/375°F/Gas 5 for 1 hour. Uncover the bird and roast for 30 minutes more. To test if the bird is done, a skewer inserted into the thickest part of the thigh meat should yield clear juices. If the juices are pink, allow a little more cooking time. Allow to cool completely. Wrap in polythene film and foil. Carve at the picnic or joint before transporting.

SERVING SUGGESTION Serve the chicken with green salad and bread sticks.

CHICKEN CASHEW SALAD

MAIN DISH   SERVES 6

1 × 15ml spoon/1 tablespoon olive oil
75g/3oz cashew nuts
½ pineapple, peeled, cored and chopped
1 cooked smoked chicken, skinned, the meat torn
into small pieces
1 large avocado, peeled, stoned and sliced into a
a little lemon juice
275g/10oz bean sprouts, rinsed
freshly ground black pepper
DRESSING
2 × 15ml spoons/2 tablespoons lemon juice
6 × 15ml spoon/6 tablespoons olive oil
1 × 5ml spoon/1 teaspoon whole grain mustard
1 × 5ml spoon/1 teaspoon clear honey
4 × 15ml spoons/4 tablespoons thick natural yogurt

Heat 1 tablespoon of oil in a heavy-based pan. Add the cashew nuts and cook, stirring continuously until golden-brown. Take care not to over-brown the nuts. Drain thoroughly on absorbent kitchen paper and place in a large mixing bowl. Add the pineapple, chicken and avocado and stir in the bean sprouts. Season with freshly ground black pepper. Turn into a sealed salad container and chill for the journey. The dressing is carried separately.

Place the lemon juice, oil, mustard and honey in a small screw-topped jar. Shake until well blended. Just before serving, blend in the yoghurt. Pour over the salad.

SERVING SUGGESTION A mixed green salad and brown rolls and butter would go well with this dish.

SEAFOOD PASTA SALAD

MAIN DISH   SERVES 4

100g/4oz multi-coloured pasta shapes
100g/4oz feta cheese, crumbled or diced
8 crab sticks, or small tin of white crab meat, drained
50g/2oz peeled prawns
2 spring onions, trimmed and finely sliced
½ green pepper, cored, de-seeded and diced
75g/3oz black olives
TOMATO DRESSING
6 × 15ml spoons/6 tablespoons olive oil
3 × 15ml spoons/3 tablespoons red wine vinegar
1 × 15ml spoon/1 tablespoon tomato purée
1 × 15ml spoon/1 teaspoon caster sugar
pinch dry mustard powder
½ × 5ml spoon/½ teaspoon lemon juice
few drops anchovy essence
1 × 15ml spoon/1 tablespoon fresh parsley, chopped

Cook the pasta shapes in boiling salted water until just tender. Refresh in cold water and drain thoroughly. Place in a large container with the cheese. Cut the crab sticks into chunks (or break tinned crab meat into pieces) and add with the prawns, onion, pepper and olives.

Whisk together the ingredients for the dressing until blended. Pour over the salad and chill for at least 1 hour before transporting.

SERVING SUGGESTION This light salad could be eaten as a main course, followed by cheese or a substantial dessert or cake.

SWEET AND SOUR CARROT SALAD

SERVES 6

350g/12oz carrots, scrubbed and grated
175g/6oz celeriac, thickly peeled and grated
SWEET AND SOUR DRESSING
4 × 15ml spoons/4 tablespoons olive oil
1 × 15ml spoon/1 tablespoon soft brown sugar
2 × 15ml spoons/2 tablespoons wine vinegar
1 × 5ml spoon/1 teaspoon soy sauce
½ × 5ml spoon/½ teaspoon Worcestershire sauce
1 × 5ml spoon/1 teaspoon clear honey
freshly-ground black pepper

Mix the grated vegetables together in a container. Whisk together the dressing ingredients and add plenty of freshly-ground black pepper. Pour the dressing over the vegetables and toss to coat thoroughly. Chill for one hour before serving.

GERMAN POTATO SALAD

SERVES 6-8

900g/2lb new potatoes, scrubbed
225g/8oz salami or pepperami sausage, cut into dice
2 × 15ml spoons/2 tablespoons fresh chives, chopped
4 hard-boiled eggs, shelled
4 × 15ml spoons/4 tablespoons thick mayonnaise
2 × 15ml spoons/2 tablespoons sour cream
salt, freshly-ground black pepper

Cook the potatoes in their skins in boiling salted water until just tender. Drain and cut in half if they are large. Allow to cool. Place in a container and mix with the salami (or sausage) and chives. Chop the eggs and add to the salad. Blend the mayonnaise and sour cream with salt and freshly-ground black pepper. Mix into the salad and chill before serving.

NEW POTATO SALAD

SERVES 6

750g/1½lb tiny new potatoes, scrubbed
3 × 15ml spoons/3 tablespoons thick mayonnaise
2 × 15ml spoons/2 tablespoons soured cream
2 × 15ml spoons/2 tablespoons fresh chives, chopped
freshly-ground black pepper
freshly-ground coriander seeds
2 hard-boiled eggs, shelled and roughly chopped

Cook the potatoes in boiling salted water until just tender. Drain and cool. Combine the mayonnaise, cream and chives and season with freshly-ground black pepper and coriander. Pour over the potatoes while they are still just warm. Toss the mixture together.

Turn the salad into the carrying container and sprinkle the eggs over the top. Chill for as long as possible before transporting.

OMELETTE SALAD

SERVES 4-6

50g/2 oz butter
6 eggs
4 × 15ml spoons/4 tablespoons water
salt, freshly-ground white pepper
4 large tomatoes
425g/15 oz tin artichoke hearts, drained
3 large cooked potatoes
1 × 15ml spoon/1 tablespoon lemon juice
1 × 15ml spoon/1 tablespoon fresh basil, chopped
1 × 15ml spoon/1 tablespoon olive oil

Melt half the butter in a 23cm/9 inch, heavy-based frying pan. Beat half the eggs with half the water and season with salt and freshly-ground white pepper. Pour into the pan when the butter starts to sizzle. Cook over high heat for a few moments, stirring with a fork. When set, slip the omelette on to a plate. Cook the remaining eggs in the same way. Roll each omelette up tightly and leave to cool.

Meanwhile, slice the tomatoes, artichokes and potatoes. Cut the omelettes into thin slices. Arrange the ingredients, overlapping, in a transportable container. Sprinkle with the lemon juice and basil and seal. Just before serving, sprinkle with the olive oil.

BROWN BREAD ICE CREAM

SERVES 6

175g/6oz brown breadcrumbs
75g/3oz soft light brown sugar
300ml/½ pint double cream
300ml/½ pint single cream
2 × 15ml spoons/2 tablespoons thick honey
2 eggs, separated
1 × 15ml spoon/1 tablespoon rum, optional

Mix the breadcrumbs and sugar thoroughly together in a large heavy-based saucepan. Heat the pan gently, stirring continuously until the sugar begins to caramelise. This may take about 10 minutes. When the mixture is crunchy and granular turn it out of the saucepan to cool on a plate.

Whip the creams together until thick. Beat the honey, egg yolks and rum together. Fold into the cream, followed by the cold crunchy crumbs. Finally, whisk the egg whites until stiff and fold into the mixture. Pour into a rigid freezing container and freeze for 2 to 3 hours until the ice cream begins to solidify round the edges of the container. Lightly beat the ice cream with a fork until it is an even texture then freeze until solid.

Spoon the frozen ice cream into a wide-necked flask to transport it to the picnic.

BRANDY SNAP CURLS

MAKES ABOUT 10

50g/2oz caster sugar
50g/2oz butter
50g/2oz golden syrup
50g/2oz plain flour, sifted
½ × 5ml spoon/½ teaspoon ground ginger
½ × 5ml spoon/½ teaspoon ground cinnamon
2 × 5ml spoons/2 teaspoons lemon juice

Place the sugar, butter and syrup in a small saucepan and melt over a gentle heat. Remove from the heat and stir in the flour, ground spices and lemon juice. Drop teaspoons of the mixture, well spaced, on baking sheets lined with non-stick baking paper. Bake, one sheet at a time, at 180°C/350°F/Gas 4 for 8 to 10 minutes until golden-brown round the edges but still pale in the centres. Quickly remove them from the oven and slide a palette knife under each before draping over a greased rolling pin. Leave them to cool so that they form curled shapes.

CREAMY PEAR AND WALNUT FLAN

SERVES 6-8

WALNUT PASTRY
225g/8oz plain flour
75g/3oz walnuts, finely ground
25g/1oz icing sugar, sifted
50g/2oz butter
2 × 15ml spoons/2 tablespoons cold water
FILLING
300ml/½ pint double cream
2 × 15ml spoons/2 tablespoons white wine
2 × 15ml spoons/2 tablespoons caster sugar
2 pears, cored, sliced
1 × 15ml spoon/1 tablespoon lemon juice
DECORATION
grated chocolate

To make the pastry, mix the flour, walnuts and icing sugar in a large bowl. Rub in the butter and stir in just enough water to mix to a firm dough. Chill, wrapped in polythene film for 30 minutes.

Roll out the pastry and line a 25cm/10inch flan tin. Cut a piece of greaseproof paper to fit the flan tin and then fill it with baking beans. Bake at 220°C/425°F/Gas 7 for 25 minutes. Remove the beans and paper and bake for a further 5 minutes. Allow to cool completely in the tin.

To make the filling, whip the cream until it begins to thicken. Add the wine and sugar and continue whipping until thick. Spoon the cream into the pastry case. Brush the pears with lemon juice and arrange on the cream.

Decorate with a sprinkling of grated chocolate. Chill for one hour. Transport the flan in the tin.

RICH CHOCOLATE SLICE

150g/5oz butter
150g/5oz caster sugar
5 eggs, separated
150g/5oz plain chocolate, melted and cooled
75g/3oz ground almonds
50g/2oz self-raising flour
FILLING
175g/6oz unsalted butter, softened
150g//5oz plain chocolate, melted
175g/6oz icing sugar, sifted
DECORATION
icing sugar

Cream together the butter and sugar until very light and fluffy. Beat in the egg yolks then stir in the melted chocolate, ground almonds and flour. Whisk the egg whites until stiff and fold into the mixture gently but evenly. Spread the mixture into a greased and lined 23 × 33cm/9 × 13inch swiss roll tin. Bake at 180°C/350°F/Gas 4 for 30 to 35 minutes. Turn the cake out onto a lightly sugared, clean tea towel and allow to cool completely.

To make the filling, mix together the butter and chocolate. Gradually stir in the icing sugar and beat until smooth.

To finish, cut the cake across into three equal pieces. Spread each piece with one third of the filling. Layer the cake to form a loaf shape. Dust the top of the cake with a little more icing sugar.

Chill before packing into a rigid container. Slice just before serving.

FRAGRANT HONEY MOUSSE

SERVES 4-6

450ml/¾ pint milk
3 eggs, separated
3 × 15ml spoons/3 tablespoons thick honey
3 × 5ml spoons/3 teaspoons gelatine
4 × 15ml spoons/4 tablespoons boiling water
250ml/8 fl oz double cream, whipped
3 passion fruit

Place the milk, egg yolks and honey in a wide bowl over a pan of simmering water. Cook gently, stirring frequently until the custard is thick enough to coat the back of a wooden spoon. Dissolve the gelatine in the boiling water and add to the custard. Remove from the heat and press a piece of polythene film over the surface of the custard to prevent a skin forming. Cool completely then fold in the double cream.

Cut the passion fruit in half and scoop the edible seeds and flesh from the fruit using a teaspoon. Add to the custard.

Finally, whisk the egg whites until stiff and fold into the mousse. Pour into individual dishes or one bowl and chill until set.

SERVING SUGGESTION Serve with a little single cream and wafer biscuits.

SUMMER SPARKLER

SERVES 6-8

8 maraschino cherries
85ml/3 fl oz cherry brandy
2 × 5ml spoons/2 teaspoons caster sugar
1 bottle rosé wine, chilled
150ml/¼ pint soda water
DECORATION
4 strawberries

Mix the cherries, brandy and sugar in a small container and seal. Have the wine and soda water well chilled before the journey. Just before serving, mix the wine and soda with the brandy mixture in a large jug. Float a few sliced strawberries on top.

A WALK IN THE COUNTRY

Exploring the countryside on foot turns an ordinary picnic into an adventure. Walkers are rewarded for their exertions by a wonderful variety of idyllic picnic spots, and once settled, the peace and fresh air make the food taste even better.

Most dishes can easily be carried in a rucksack and some of the more manageable snacks could be packed at the top for munching along the way – like the Pork and Cranberry Samosas and Garlic Tortilla in Pitta Bread, for example.

Pack a fair amount of substantial food: if it's a wintry day the Hearty Bean Soup makes a warming surprise and can easily be transported in a wide-necked flask. Follow with Chicken and Veal Terrine perhaps, or Spiced Meatballs served with a dip.

Cakes and pastries make a good excuse for a stop around tea-time. The mention of Flaky Cheese and Apple Strudel, Apricot and Walnut Slice and Choc-nut Rocks will have most people reaching for their rucksacks.

TARAMASALATA

APPETIZER   SERVES 6-8

225g/8 oz smoked cod's roe, skinned
4 slices white bread, crusts removed
4 × 15ml spoons/4 tablespoons milk
1 shallot, peeled and finely chopped
75ml/3 fl oz olive oil
120ml/4 fl oz salad oil
1 large lemon, juice only
freshly-ground white pepper

Taste the cod's roe for saltiness. If it is very salty, soak it in cold water for about an hour. Drain and place in a food processor. Pour the milk over the bread and then add to the cod's roe with the shallot. Work until a smooth paste is formed. While the machine is working, gradually pour in the oil very slowly, followed by the lemon juice. Season with ground white pepper.

Pack into individual containers.

SERVING SUGGESTION   Serve with black olives and strips of pitta bread for dunking.

POTTED STILTON

APPETIZER   SERVES 6

75g/3 oz unsalted butter
225g/8 oz Stilton cheese, rind removed, crumbled
2 × 15ml spoons/2 tablespoons port
50g/2 oz walnuts, roughly chopped
¼ × 5ml spoon/¼ teaspoon cayenne pepper

Work 50g/2 oz of the butter into the crumbled Stilton using a wooden spoon. Mix until thoroughly blended. Stir in the port, nuts and cayenne pepper. Taste to check for seasoning.

Pack the mixture into small terrine pots or pâté dishes (or perhaps, small waxed-paper containers.) Melt the remaining butter, strain it through scalded muslin and pour over the potted Stilton to seal. Allow to cool and set. Serve with crackers and celery.

VARIATION   *Potted Danish Blue*
Make as for the Potted Stilton but use a blue-veined Danish cheese. Add a pinch of celery seeds to the mixture before potting.

PORK AND CRANBERRY SAMOSAS

APPETIZER   MAKES 12

25g/1oz butter
1 × 15ml spoon/1 tablespoon oil
1 onion, peeled and chopped
225g/8oz pork fillet, trimmed and diced
300ml/½ pint white stock
1 × 15ml spoon/1 tablespoon Worcestershire sauce
100g/4oz fresh, or frozen and thawed, cranberries
12 sheets filo pastry
75g/3oz butter, melted

Melt the 25g/1oz of butter in a large pan with the oil and fry the onion for 2 minutes. Add the pork fillet and cook for 10 minutes. Add the stock, freshly-ground black pepper and Worcestershire sauce. Cover and simmer for 1 hour. Stir in the cranberries and heat through. Remove from the heat.

Work with one sheet of pastry at a time. Keep the rest damp under a rinsed and wrung-out tea towel. Brush one sheet of pastry with the melted butter. Fold the top third, lengthways, down over the centre third and the bottom third up over the centre. Brush the strip with butter. Place a spoonful of the meat mixture at one end of the strip. Fold the end of the strip over the filling diagonally to make a triangle. Continue folding the pastry over the filling, working your way along the strip to finish with a neat triangular parcel. Brush again with butter and place on a baking sheet. Repeat the process to make 12 parcels. Bake at 220°C/425°F/Gas 7 for 15 to 20 minutes until golden. Allow to cool on a wire rack. Pack in a rigid container.

VARIATION *Sagey Pork Parcels*
Make as for the Pork and Cranberry Samosas but instead of cranberries, substitute a large peeled and finely-chopped cooking apple plus 1 × 15ml spoon/1 tablespoon of fresh chopped sage.

CREAMY MUSHROOM PUFFS

APPETIZER   MAKES 16

150ml/¼ pint water
50g/2oz butter
65g/2½oz plain flour
½ × 5ml spoon/½ teaspoon dry mustard
2 eggs, beaten
FILLING
25g/1oz butter
1 clove garlic, peeled and crushed
1 small onion, peeled and chopped
1 × 15ml spoon/1 tablespoon fresh parsley, chopped
100g/4oz button mushrooms, chopped
75g/3oz cream cheese
2 × 15ml spoons/2 tablespoons thick Greek yoghurt
pinch cayenne pepper
1 × 5ml spoon/1 teaspoon lemon juice
GARNISH
paprika pepper

Place the water and butter in a pan. Heat until the butter melts. Bring to the boil and quickly add the flour and mustard. Beat well, over the heat for 1 minute. Allow to cool for a few minutes. Gradually beat in sufficient egg to form a smooth glossy paste that will just hold its shape.

Spoon the mixture into a piping bag fitted with a large plain nozzle and pipe 16 small rounds on greased baking sheets. Bake at 220°C/425°F/Gas 7 for 25 to 30 minutes until very crisp. Cool on a wire rack.

To make the filling, melt the butter in a pan and fry the garlic and onion for 2 minutes. Add the parsley and mushrooms and cook for 5 minutes. Allow to cool. Blend together the cheese, yoghurt, pepper and lemon juice in a bowl. Season and stir in the mushroom mixture. Chill.

Just before packing, split the puffs and fill them with the mixture. Dust with a little paprika pepper and pack the puffs into rigid containers.

VEGETABLE STICKS WITH BLUE CHEESE DIP

APPETIZER   SERVES 4-6

DIP
1 egg yolk
2 × 5ml spoons/2 teaspoons white wine vinegar
pinch mustard powder
salt, freshly-ground white pepper
150ml/¼ pint olive oil
2 × 5ml spoons/2 teaspoons boiling water
1 × 5ml spoon/1 teaspoon lemon juice
50g/2oz curd cheese
50g/2oz Danish blue cheese, crumbled
TO SERVE
celery, carrots, cucumber and peppers cut into sticks

Place the egg yolk in a bowl with the vinegar, mustard and a little salt and freshly ground white pepper. Whisk together. Gradually whisk in the olive oil, drop by drop at first, until it is all absorbed and the mixture is thick and shiny. Whisk in the boiling water and lemon juice. Blend the cheeses together and stir evenly through the dip.

Serve in small sealed containers. Wrap the vegetable sticks in polythene film and chill well before packing.

FRESH TOMATO CHUTNEY

SERVES 6

6 ripe tomatoes
1 onion, peeled and finely chopped
1 lime, finely grated rind and juice
2 × 15ml spoons/2 tablespoons fresh mint or coriander, chopped
few drops Tabasco sauce

Plunge the tomatoes in boiling water for 10 seconds. Drain and peel away the skins. Cut in half and remove the seeds and tough stalk base. Chop the flesh finely. Mix with the remaining ingredients and check the seasoning for salt. Pack into small pots and serve with the terrine.

HEARTY BEAN SOUP

MAIN DISH   SERVES 6

50g/2oz red kidney beans
50g/2oz haricot beans
50g/2oz flageolet beans
50g/2oz pinto beans
1 × 15ml spoon/1 tablespoon oil
3 rashers streaky bacon, derinded, chopped
1 large onion, peeled and chopped
2 sticks celery, chopped
1.4 litres/2½ pints stock
400g/14oz tin chopped tomatoes
1 × 5ml spoon/1 teaspoon dried mixed herbs
1 × 5ml spoon/1 teaspoon Worcestershire sauce
freshly-ground black pepper, salt
3 × 15ml spoons/3 tablespoons fresh parsley,
chopped

Soak all the beans together in a large bowl of cold water overnight. Drain and rinse thoroughly. Cover with fresh water and bring to the boil. Boil rapidly for 10 minutes then simmer for 1 hour.

Heat the oil in a large pan. Fry the bacon, onion and celery for 5 minutes. Drain the beans and add to the pan with the stock, tomatoes, herbs and Worcestershire sauce. Season with freshly-ground black pepper. Do not add salt at this stage as it toughens the beans. Simmer for 1 hour.

Add the parsley and season with a little salt if desired. Transport in wide-necked flasks.

SERVING SUGGESTION Pitta bread, split and stuffed with green salad and sliced onions would make a good, substantial meal with this soup.

CHICKEN AND VEAL TERRINE

MAIN DISH   SERVES 6-8

450g/1lb chicken breasts, skinned, boned and finely
chopped
100g/4oz cooked long grain rice
½ × 5ml spoon/½ teaspoon mixed spice
pinch ground mace
25g/1oz butter
50g/2oz button mushrooms, chopped
2 sticks celery, chopped
100g/4oz curd cheese
150ml/¼ pint milk
1 egg white
1 × 15ml spoon/1 tablespoon lemon juice
freshly-ground white pepper
2 veal escalopes, approximately 100g/4oz each
2 bunches watercress, trimmed and finely chopped
75g/3oz stuffed green olives, chopped

Place the chicken, rice, spice and mace in a food processor and blend until very smooth. Cover and place in the freezer for 30 minutes.

Melt the butter in a frying pan and cook the mushrooms and celery for 5 minutes. Drain, cool and put aside.

Blend the curd cheese and milk until smooth. Whisk the egg white stiffly and fold in. Gently fold the cheese mixture into the chicken mixture.

Stir the lemon juice into the mushroom mixture. Season with freshly-ground white pepper.

Place the veal slices between two sheets of polythene film and beat out very thinly. Mix together the watercress and olives. Spoon half the chicken mixture into a greased 900g/2lb loaf tin.

Lay the veal out to make a strip as long as the tin. Place the watercress mixture along one long edge and roll the veal up to make a long tube. Place this down the centre of the half-filled tin and carefully spoon the remaining chicken mixture on top. Knock the tin sharply on the work surface to settle the contents. Cover and place in a roasting tin filled with 2.5cm/1 inch boiling water. Bake at 200°C/400°F/Gas 6 for 1¼ hours.

Cool in the tin. Turn out and wrap in polythene film and foil before packing and slice before serving. Alternatively, cut slices of terrine before leaving home and wrap individually.

GARLIC TORTILLA IN PITTA BREADS

MAIN DISH   SERVES 4

50g/2oz butter
1-2 cloves garlic, peeled and crushed
1 onion, peeled and sliced
350g/12oz cooked potato, diced
75g/3oz cooked ham, chopped
4 eggs
2 × 5ml spoons/2 teaspoons cold water
salt, freshly-ground black pepper
2 × 15ml spoons/2 tablespoons fresh parsley,
chopped
4 wholemeal pitta breads, split and buttered
crisp lettuce

Heat the butter in a deep frying pan. Add the garlic and onion and cook for 2 minutes. Add the potato and ham and cook for a further 10 minutes. Beat the eggs with the water and season with salt and ground black pepper. Whisk in the parsley. Pour the egg mixture over the vegetables. Allow to cook slowly for 10 to 15 minutes over a low heat until set. Turn out on to a board and allow to cool.

Cut into eight wedges and slip these into the pitta bread pockets. Add pieces of crisp lettuce and wrap individually in foil.

Small, ripe tomatoes are good with these.

SPICED MEATBALLS AND DIP

MAIN DISH   SERVES 4-6

25g/1oz fresh white breadcrumbs
225g/8oz lean beef, minced
1 egg, beaten
½ × 5ml spoon/½ teaspoon *garam marsala* powder
½ × 5ml spoon/½ teaspoon ground allspice
1 × 5ml spoon/1 teaspoon fresh chives, chopped
1 × 5ml spoon/1 teaspoon fresh parsley, chopped
oil for shallow frying
DIP
300ml/½ pint thick Greek yoghurt
150ml/¼ pint sieved canned tomatoes
few drops Tabasco sauce
½ × 5ml spoon/½ teaspoon Worcestershire sauce
2 × 15ml spoons/2 tablespoons fresh parsley,
chopped
salt, freshly-ground black pepper

Mix together the breadcrumbs, beef, egg, spices and herbs. Knead with the hands to a smooth mixture. Form into 24 small balls. Cover and chill for 1 hour. Heat the oil and fry the meatballs for 10 minutes, turning occasionally. Drain thoroughly on absorbent kitchen paper. When cool, pack into small individual containers with cocktail sticks for spearing.

To make the dip, blend together all the ingredients and season well with salt and freshly-ground black pepper. Pack into small sealed containers and chill before transporting.

PEPPERY CHICKEN PARCELS

MAIN DISH   MAKES 6

6 chicken breasts, skinned and boned
75g/3oz cream cheese
75g/3oz curd cheese
1½ × 15ml spoons/1½ tablespoons tomato purée
1 × 5ml spoon/1 teaspoon pink or green
peppercorns, drained and crushed
1 × 5ml spoon/1 teaspoon fresh oregano, chopped
few drops Tabasco sauce
1 tinned red pimiento, drained and finely chopped
350g/12oz prepared puff pastry
1 egg, beaten
2 × 15ml spoons/2 tablespoons sesame seeds

Place the chicken breasts between two sheets of
polythene film. Beat with a rolling pin to flatten
the meat evenly. Beat together the cheeses,
tomato purée, peppercorns, oregano and Tabasco.
Divide this mixture into six portions and spread
evenly over the chicken breasts. Sprinkle the
chopped pimiento over the filling. Roll each
chicken breast up from the pointed end, wrap in
polythene film and chill for 30 minutes.

Divide the pastry into 6 pieces and roll each
piece out thinly to a rectangle 3 times as wide as
the chicken rolls. Unwrap the rolls. Brush the
edges of the pastry with beaten egg and enclose
each chicken roll in pastry. Place on a baking sheet
with the join underneath.

Brush the parcels with beaten egg and slash the
pastry with a knife to decorate. Sprinkle with
sesame seeds. Bake at 220°C/425°F/Gas 7 for 25
minutes until golden-brown. Allow to cool on a
wire rack.

Pack in a rigid container for transporting.

SERVING SUGGESTION For a substantial meal,
serve Chicken Parcels with a coleslaw salad and
follow with cheese and crackers or a light creamy
dessert.

APRICOT BRANDY CREAM MOUSSE

SERVES 4-6

1 × 15ml spoon/1 tablespoon gelatine
3 × 15ml spoons/3 tablespoons boiling water
2 eggs, separated
50g/2oz caster sugar
3 × 15ml spoons/3 tablespoons apricot brandy
150ml/¼ pint cream

Dissolve the gelatine in boiling water. Place the egg yolks, sugar and brandy in a wide bowl over a pan of simmering water. Whisk for 5 to 10 minutes until the mixture is thick and foamy. Whisk the dissolved gelatine into the egg and sugar mixture. Remove from the heat and continue to whisk until cool.

Whip the cream until thick and fold in. Whisk the egg whites stiffly and fold in. Spoon into individual containers and chill until set.

FLAKY CHEESE AND APPLE STRUDEL

MAKES 18 SLICES

DOUGH
85ml/3fl oz warm water
1 egg, beaten
15g/½oz butter, melted
200g/7oz strong plain flour
pinch of salt
FILLING
100g/4oz cottage cheese, sieved
100g/4oz cream cheese, softened
2 egg yolks
1 lemon, finely grated rind only
1 × 15ml spoon/1 tablespoon semolina
2 × 15ml spoons/2 tablespoons hazelnuts, finely ground
75g/3oz soft brown sugar
50g/2oz sultanas
100g/4oz butter, melted
100g/4oz fresh white breadcrumbs
3 cooking apples, peeled, cored and thinly sliced
1 × 5ml spoon/1 teaspoon ground mixed spice

To make the dough, beat together the water, egg and melted butter. Mix this into the flour and salt to make a dough. Knead well for about 10 minutes until the dough is soft, smooth and elastic. Wrap in polythene film and leave to relax for 30 minutes.

To make the filling, beat together the cottage cheese, cream cheese and egg yolks. Work in the lemon rind, semolina, nuts and sugar. Stir in the sultanas.

Smooth a large, clean cloth over the work surface. Dust lightly with flour and roll out the dough on this as thinly as possible. Then pull the dough out very gently with your hands until it is very thin and almost transparent. Trim the edges square with scissors. Brush all over with the melted butter and sprinkle with breadcrumbs. Spread the cheese mixture over this and arrange the apple slices evenly on top. Sprinkle with the spice.

Roll up the dough from a short side with the help of the cloth. Bend the roll into a horseshoe shape so that it will fit on to a large greased baking sheet.

Bake at 230°C/450°F/Gas 8 for 10 minutes then reduce the heat to 200°C/400°F/Gas 6 for a further 20 minutes. Allow to cool. Cut into slices and pack interleaved with greaseproof paper.

APPLE AND ALMOND DANISH PASTRIES

MAKES 8

225g/8 oz strong plain flour
pinch of salt
15g/½ oz fresh yeast
135ml/4 fl oz milk, warmed slightly
½ egg
25g/1 oz butter, melted
75g/3 oz butter, chilled
FILLING
50g/2 oz caster sugar
50g/2 oz butter
50g/2 oz ground almonds
4 × 15ml spoons/4 tablespoons apple purée
4 × 15ml spoons/4 tablespoons apricot jam, warmed

Sift the flour and salt together into a warmed bowl. Blend the yeast and the milk. Whisk in the egg and melted butter. Add these liquids to the flour and mix to a smooth dough with a wooden spoon. Knead for 10 minutes until the dough is soft, silky and elastic. Leave to rest in the refrigerator in an oiled polythene bag for 15 minutes. Punch the dough to knock out the air and knead once more until smooth. Roll out on a lightly floured surface to a long rectangle.

Divide the chilled butter in half. Using half the butter, dot small flakes of it over the top two-thirds of the dough. Fold up the bottom third over the centre and the top third down on top of them. Press the edges of the dough to seal and cover with polythene film. Chill for 20 minutes. Give the dough a quarter turn, clockwise. Roll out to the same size as before. Dot with the remaining butter and repeat the process. Fold and roll twice more. Leave the dough to rest in the refrigerator for at least 4 hours.

Roll out the dough to about 6mm/¼ inch thick in a rectangle of 20 × 35cm/8 × 16 inches. Cut into 2 rows of 4 squares. Beat the filling ingredients together. Place a spoonful on the centre of each square. Bring two opposite corners up over the filling and press down to seal. Leave the pastries to rise on a greased baking sheet in a warm place, covered in oiled polythene film. Remove film and bake at 220°C/425°F/Gas 7 for 10 to 12 minutes. Brush with jam and cool on a wire rack.

Pack into rigid containers.

GINGERED ALMOND LOAF

SERVES 8-10

100g/4 oz butter
100g/4 oz caster sugar
2 eggs, beaten
175g/6 oz self-raising flour
50g/2 oz ground almonds
50g/2 oz stem ginger, chopped
DECORATION
25g/1 oz stem ginger, chopped

Cream the butter and sugar together until light and fluffy. Gradually beat in the eggs, creaming well after each addition. Fold in the flour and almonds and stir in the ginger. Turn into a greased and lined 900g/2 lb loaf tin and sprinkle the remaining stem ginger over the top.

Bake at 180°C/350°F/Gas 4 for 45 to 50 minutes. When a skewer inserted comes out cleanly the cake is done. Cool in the tin for 10 minutes then turn onto a wire rack.

Pack, cut into slices and buttered if liked.

VARIATION *Apricot and Walnut Slice*
Make as for the Gingered Almond Loaf but substitute 100g/4 oz chopped dried apricots for the ginger and chopped walnuts for the ground almonds. Decorate with chopped dried apricots.

CHOC-NUT ROCKS

MAKES 12

50g/2oz butter
50g/2oz golden syrup
150g/5oz packet chocolate finger biscuits, chopped
50g/2oz sultanas
50g/2oz walnuts, chopped

Melt the butter and syrup together in a pan over gentle heat. Stir in the remaining ingredients. Turn into a greased, lined 900g/2lb loaf tin. Press down and chill until set.

Turn out and cut into 12 small triangles. Wrap individually in foil and keep as cool as possible before and during transporting.

FRUITED FLAPJACK

MAKES 12 FINGERS

100g/4oz dried apricots
50g/2oz dried peaches
100g/4oz dried bananas
50g/2oz sultanas
2 oranges, finely grated rind and juice
250g/9oz rolled oats
250g/9oz wholemeal flour
150g/5oz demerara sugar
200g/7oz butter
2 × 15ml spoons/2 tablespoons golden syrup

Place the dried fruits, orange rind and juice in a pan and bring to the boil. Simmer gently, stirring frequently for 5 minutes until softened. Cool and put aside. Mix the oats and flour in a large bowl. Place the sugar, butter and syrup in a pan and melt together. Pour onto the oats and flour and mix in. Spread half the oats mixture into the base of a greased and lined 18 × 28cm/7 × 11 inch flan tin. Spread the dried fruit mixture evenly over this and top with the remaining oat mixture. Press down firmly.

Bake at 190°C/375°F/Gas 5 for 25 to 30 minutes until golden-brown. Mark into fingers and cool in the tin. Turn out and cut up.

Pack, interleaved with greaseproof paper, in a rigid container.

LEMON APRICOT CHEESECAKE

SERVES 4-6

225g/8oz chocolate digestive biscuits, crushed
75g/3oz butter
FILLING
225g/8oz cream cheese
100g/4oz caster sugar
2 eggs, separated
1 lemon, grated rind and juice
1 small tin apricots in natural juice, chopped and drained
15g/½oz gelatine, dissolved in 3 × 15 ml spoons/
3 tablespoons boiling water
150ml/¼ pint double cream
DECORATION
strips of lemon zest

Place the biscuits in a bowl. Melt the butter and pour over the biscuits. Mix until evenly blended. Press the mixture into the base of an oiled, loose-based 20cm/8inch cake tin. Chill until set firm. To make the filling, beat the cheese with the sugar, egg yolks, lemon rind and juice until smooth. Stir in the apricots and cooled gelatine. Whip the cream and fold in. Finally, whisk the egg whites stiffly and gently fold in. Pour the filling on to the biscuit base and chill until set. Transport in the tin. To release the cheesecake slip a knife round the outside of the tin. Decorate with lemon strips and serve on the tin base with single cream.

HOMEMADE LEMONADE

SERVES 6-8

1 lemon
275g/10oz sugar
1 × 5ml spoon/1 teaspoon cream of tartar
boiling water

Wash the lemon in hot water to release the oils in the rind. Thinly pare the rind into a bowl. Add the cream of tartar and the sugar. Pour on just enough boiling water to cover. Stir to dissolve the sugar. Add the juice of the lemon. Allow to stand, covered for 24 hours. Serve diluted to taste, with iced water. Either keep chilled in a flask or on a hot day try freezing the diluted drink in a plastic bottle not filled quite to the top. Pack the frozen drink and it will have just melted and be ice cool by lunchtime!

SUMMER INTERLUDE

A hot summer afternoon is best spent out-of-doors, in the shade of an overhanging tree, cooled by a light breeze. A lunchtime picnic is the perfect excuse for this. Choose a spot, open the hamper and prepare for a leisurely afternoon.

With a little invention and patience even the most fragile dishes can be successfully packed and transported. The Seafood Cocktail, which is served cupped in a crisp curl of lettuce, travels well and makes an attractive appetizer.

Cool salads and delicately-flavoured fish ideas tantalize the lazy mid-summer appetite. Creamy Apple and Horseradish Chicken with Mixed Wild Rice Salad and Rosemary Bread Sticks could be served to a party of hearty eaters, while tempting snacks like Olive and Anchovy Bread satisfy the whims of casual nibblers. Finish the picnic with chilled Kiwi Citrus Fruit Salad or ice-cold Cassata.

SEAFOOD COCKTAILS

APPETIZER   SERVES 8

1 iceberg lettuce heart
3 sticks celery, thinly sliced
100g/4 oz shelled prawns
225g/8 oz light and dark crabmeat, thawed if frozen
200g/7 oz tin tuna in brine, drained and flaked
SAUCE
150ml/¼ pint mayonnaise
4 × 15ml spoons/4 tablespoons thick Greek yoghurt
1 × 15ml spoon/1 tablespoon tomato purée
150ml/¼ pint whipping cream, whipped
1 tablespoon lemon juice
few drops Tabasco sauce
few drops Worcestershire sauce
freshly-ground white pepper
GARNISH
lemon slices
mustard and cress

Separate the lettuce heart carefully into small leaves that curl to form a cup shape. Chill them in a sealed container. Mix the celery, prawns, crabmeat and tuna. In another bowl combine the mayonnaise, yoghurt, tomato purée, cream, lemon juice, Tabasco and Worcestershire sauce. Season with freshly-ground white pepper. Mix the sauce with the fish and spoon the mixture into the lettuce cups. Pack them close together in a container garnished with the lemon slices and cress. Chill before transporting. These are picked up and eaten with the fingers.

TRICOLOUR VEGETABLE TERRINE .

APPETIZER   SERVES 8   ·

450g/1 lb carrots, peeled and chopped
175g/6 oz potatoes, peeled and chopped
½ cauliflower, cut into florets
1 orange, grated rind and juice
25g/1 oz Emmental cheese, grated
1 bunch watercress, trimmed and chopped
450g/1 lb frozen chopped spinach, thawed,
well-drained
25g/1 oz gelatine
150ml/¼ pint boiling chicken stock or water
4 × 15ml spoons/4 tablespoons mayonnaise
3 egg whites, stiffly beaten

Steam the carrots, potatoes and cauliflower separately until tender. Drain. Purée the carrots in a blender or food processor together with the orange rind and juice. Purée the potatoes and cauliflower with the cheese. Purée the watercress and spinach together. Season each mixture.

Dissolve the gelatine in the stock or water and cool. Divide the dissolved gelatine, mayonnaise and egg whites equally between the three purées. Spoon the carrot mixture into the base of a greased and lined 900g/2 lb loaf tin or terrine. Chill in the freezer until set. Spoon the cauliflower purée on top and chill until set. Finally top with the watercress purée and chill in the refrigerator until completely set.

Cover and transport in the terrine. Turn out just before serving and cut into slices. Alternatively, cut the terrine into slices at home and wrap individually.

SERVING SUGGESTION   Greek salad and Saffron bread would make a substantial meal with the terrine.

MUSHROOM TART

APPETIZER   SERVES 4-6

PASTRY
50g/2oz butter
100g/4oz self-raising wholemeal flour
1 × 15ml spoon/1 tablespoon Parmesan cheese,
finely grated
1 × 5ml spoon/1 teaspoon wholegrain mustard
2-3 × 15ml spoons/2-3 tablespoons iced water
FILLING
50g/2oz butter
1 onion, peeled and sliced
1 clove garlic, peeled and crushed
225g/8oz button mushrooms, sliced
2 eggs, beaten
150ml/¼ pint double cream
1 × 5ml spoon/1 teaspoon coriander seeds,
freshly-ground
50g/2oz Gruyère cheese, grated
freshly-ground white pepper

To make the pastry, rub the butter into the flour. Mix in the Parmesan and mustard and just enough water to form a firm dough. Wrap in polythene film and chill for 20 minutes.

To make the filling, melt the butter in a large shallow pan and fry the onion and garlic for 2 minutes. Add the mushrooms and cook for 5 minutes. Beat together the eggs, cream and coriander. Season with freshly-ground white pepper.

Roll out the pastry on a lightly floured work surface. Use to line a 20cm/8 inch flan dish or tin. Set on a baking sheet. Spoon the cooked mushroom mixture into the flan and pour over the eggs. Scatter the cheese over the top and bake at 180°C/350°F/Gas 4 for 25 to 30 minutes until set and golden-brown. Cool and transport in the dish or tin. Cut into slices to serve.

PRAWN AND ASPARAGUS MOUSSE

APPETIZER   SERVES 6-8

2 350g/12oz cans asparagus spears, drained
120ml/4 fl oz thick Greek yoghurt
4 × 15ml spoons/4 tablespoons mayonnaise
50g/2oz curd cheese
100g/4oz cream cheese
4 × 5ml spoons/4 teaspoons gelatine
4 × 15ml spoons/4 tablespoons boiling water
1 × 15ml spoon/1 tablespoon lemon juice
few drops Tabasco sauce
¼ × 5ml spoon/¼ teaspoon paprika pepper
2 × 15ml spoons/2 tablespoons fresh parsley,
chopped
100g/4oz cooked, shelled prawns
freshly-ground white pepper

Place the asparagus, yoghurt, mayonnaise and cheeses in a liquidiser or food processor. Blend to a smooth purée. Sprinkle the gelatine over the boiling water in a small bowl and stir until dissolved. Cool. Add to the asparagus cream with the lemon juice, Tabasco, paprika and parsley. Season with freshly-ground white pepper. Stir in the prawns and pour into a container for transporting. Chill until set.

SERVING SUGGESTION Serve the mousse in scoops with green or mixed salad.

SALMON AND LEMON TERRINE

MAIN DISH   SERVES 8-10

450g/1 lb fillets of plaice, skinned and cut into pieces
75g/3 oz fresh white breadcrumbs
2 lemons, grated rind of both, juice of one
85ml/3 fl oz dry white wine
150ml/¼ pint single cream
freshly-ground white pepper
25g/1 oz butter
2 × 15ml spoons/2 tablespoons fresh dill, chopped
2 × 15ml spoons/2 tablespoons fresh parsley,
chopped
1 × 15ml spoon/1 tablespoon fresh chives, chopped
225g/8 oz strip fresh salmon fillet

Place the plaice, breadcrumbs, lemon rind and
juice, wine and cream in a food processor and
work until quite smooth. Season with freshly-
ground white pepper. Chill for 1 hour.

Thoroughly coat the inside of a 900g/2 lb loaf tin
or terrine with the butter. Place the herbs in the tin
and tip the tin in all directions to coat the sides
and base completely with herbs.

Spoon half the fish purée into the prepared tin
and lay the piece of salmon along it. Spoon in the
remaining fish purée and smooth the top. Tap the
tin on the work surface to settle the contents.

Cover and stand in a roasting tin half-filled with
boiling water. Bake at 200°C/400°F/Gas 6 for 1
hour. Cool and transport in the tin. Serve in slices.
Alternatively, the terrine can be cut into slices
before leaving home and individually wrapped in
film or foil.

SERVING SUGGESTION Serve the terrine with
New Potato Salad (page 16) and coleslaw.

CREAMY APPLE AND HORSERADISH CHICKEN

MAIN DISH   SERVES 6-8

1 boiling fowl (approximately 1.6kg/3½ lb)
bouquet garni
2 cooking apples, peeled, cored and sliced
300ml/½ pint mayonniase
2-3 × 5ml spoons/2-3 teaspoons fresh horseradish,
grated
150ml/¼ pint whipping cream, whipped

Wash the bird inside and out. Place in a large pan with the bouquet garni and cover with cold water. Cover, bring to the boil and simmer for about 1 hour, or until tender. Reserve a little of the stock and drain the bird. Allow to cool. Remove and discard the skin and bones and cut the flesh into bite-sized pieces.

Place the apples in a pan with 2 × 15ml spoons/2 tablespoons of the reserved stock and simmer until reduced to a thick purée. Cool. Stir into the mayonnaise with the horseradish and whipped cream. Stir in the chicken and chill before serving.

Transport the chicken in a shallow container and keep as cool as possible.

SERVING SUGGESTION Mixed Wild Rice Salad and Rosemary Bread Sticks would go well with this dish.

RAISED CHICKEN AND HAM PIE

MAIN DISH   SERVES 8-10

700g/1½ lb plain flour
2 × 5ml spoons/2 teaspoons salt
100g/4 oz lard
50g/2 oz butter
300ml/½ pint water
FILLING
450g/1 lb cooked chicken, skin and bones removed
450g/1 lb cooked gammon joint, rind removed
1 onion, peeled and chopped
3 × 15ml spoons/3 tablespoons mild wholegrain
mustard
½ × 5ml spoon/½ teaspoon ground mace
salt, freshly-ground black pepper
1 egg, beaten
2 × 5ml spoons/2 teaspoons gelatine
300ml/½ pint boiling chicken stock
3 × 15ml spoons/3 tablespoons fresh parsley,
chopped

Sift the flour and salt into a mixing bowl and make a well in the centre. Place the lard, butter and water in a small pan. Heat until melted then bring to the boil. Pour into the flour and quickly mix to a fairly soft dough. Turn out on to a lightly floured work surface and knead until smooth.

Reserve one quarter of the pastry and put aside, covered, in a warm place. Use the remaining pastry to line the base and sides of a large raised pie mould. Slice the chicken and ham and layer this into the lined mould, scattering the layers with the onion, mustard and mace. Season with salt and freshly-ground black pepper. Roll out the reserved pastry and use to make a lid and cover the pie. Dampen the edges to seal. Trim, crimp the crusts and decorate with the trimmings. Cut a 9mm/ ⅜ inch hole in the centre of the lid. Brush the lid and decorations with beaten egg. Bake at 200°C/ 400°F/Gas 6 for 30 minutes. Brush again with beaten egg and reduce the oven temperature to 170°C/325°F/Gas 3 for 45 minutes until golden-brown.

Dissolve the gelatine in the stock, check the seasoning and stir in the parsley. As the pie cools, pour in the stock through the hole in the lid using a small funnel. Chill overnight.

Transport the pie in the tin. Serve in slices with salad.

MIXED WILD RICE SALAD

SERVES 6-8

25g/1 oz wild rice
75g/3 oz long grain rice
1 red pepper, cored, deseeded and diced
100g/4 oz sweetcorn kernels
100g/4 oz green beans, cooked
DRESSING
2 × 15ml spoons/2 tablespoons lemon juice
4 × 15ml spoons/4 tablespoons olive oil
2 × 15ml spoons/2 tablespoons fresh parsley,
chopped
1 × 15ml spoon/1 tablespoon fresh chives, chopped
pinch of sugar
pinch of ground mace
1 × 5ml spoon/1 teaspoon wholegrain mustard
freshly-ground black pepper

Pour boiling water over the wild rice to cover.
Leave standing for 2 to 3 minutes. Drain. Cook all
the rice together in plenty of boiling salted water
until tender – about 12 minutes. Drain and rinse in
cold water. Mix in the pepper, sweetcorn and
beans. Place all the dressing ingredients in a small
screw-topped jar and shake together until well
blended. Add freshly-ground black pepper and
pour over the rice. Toss to coat.

Transport the salad in a sealed container.

SALAD NIÇOISE

SERVES 6-8

75g/3 oz french beans, cooked until tender
2 large potatoes, peeled, cooked and cut into pieces
4 hard-boiled eggs, shelled and cut into wedges
4 ripe tomatoes, chopped
50g/2 oz black olives
425g/14 oz tin tuna in brine, drained
15g/½ oz tin anchovies, drained
DRESSING
3 × 15ml spoons/3 tablespoons olive oil
1 × 15ml spoon/1 tablespoon white wine vinegar
pinch of sugar
pinch of salt
pinch of mustard powder
¼ × 5ml spoon/¼ teaspoon dried mixed herbs
1 × 5ml spoon/1 teaspoon lemon juice

Combine the beans, potatoes, eggs, tomatoes,
olives and tuna. Arrange the anchovy fillets, cut
into strips, over the salad. Transport in a sealed
container. Put the dressing ingredients in a small
lidded jar and transport separately. Shake to blend
and pour over the salad just before serving.

GREEK SALAD

SERVES 6

1 crisp-leafed lettuce
¼ white cabbage, finely shredded
4 tomatoes, cubed
½ cucumber, cubed
100g/4oz black olives
100g/4oz feta cheese

DRESSING
6 × 15ml spoons/6 tablespoons olive oil
1 × 15ml spoon/1 tablespoon wine vinegar
¼ × 5ml spoon/¼ teaspoon sugar
1 × 5ml spoon/1 teaspoon fresh basil or oregano,
chopped

Combine the lettuce, torn into pieces, cabbage, tomatoes and cucumber in a large container. Sprinkle over the olives and cheese. Chill thoroughly.

Whisk the dressing ingredients together and put into a screw-topped jar. Dress the salad just before serving.

MOZZARELLA AND TOMATO SALAD

SERVES 6-8

2 175g/6oz Mozzarella cheeses
4 sweet, ripe Spanish tomatoes
8 black peppercorns, crushed
10 small fresh basil leaves
salt, olive oil for dressing

Slice the cheeses and the tomatoes and arrange them in a container, overlapping, in circles. Sprinkle over the peppercorns, olives and basil. Cover.

Just before serving season with a little salt and sprinkle with olive oil.

KIWI CITRUS FRUIT SALAD

SERVES 6-8

4 oranges, peeled, segmented, all pith removed
1 grapefruit, peeled, segmented, all pith removed
4 kiwi fruit, peeled and sliced
1 lime, grated rind and juice
50g/2oz caster sugar
150ml/¼ pint water
1-2 × 15ml spoons/1-2 tablespoons kirsch liqueur
few drops rose water

Mix the orange, grapefruit and kiwi fruit. Place the lime rind and juice, sugar and water in a small pan. Heat gently to dissolve the sugar and bring to the boil for 2 minutes. Cool and stir in the kirsch and a few drops of rose water. Pour over the fruit and chill. Transport in a sealed container.

CASSATA

SERVES 6-8

300ml/½ pint milk
300ml/½ pint double cream
4 egg yolks
100g/4oz caster sugar
150ml/¼ pint double cream, whipped
1 orange, grated rind and juice
few drops orange colouring
25g/1oz raisins
25g/1oz candied peel, chopped
25g/1oz glacé cherries, chopped
2 × 15ml spoons/2 tablespoons Madeira wine
75ml/3fl oz raspberry sorbet

Bring the milk and double cream to the boil and remove from the heat. Whisk the egg yolks and sugar together until thick and light. Stir in the scalded milk and cream. Set over a pan of simmering water and cook, stirring frequently until the mixture has thickened enough to coat the back of a wooden spoon. Remove from the heat and cover the surface of the custard with polythene film to prevent a skin forming. Leave until cold.

Fold the whipped cream into the custard and then reserve one third of the mixture. To the remainder, add the orange rind and juice and a few drops of colouring. Add the raisins, peel, cherries and Madeira wine to the reserved portion. Freeze separately until mushy. Beat until smooth and refreeze. Soften the orange ice cream and spread it round the sides of a chilled metal mould or basin lined with polythene film. Freeze until firm. Soften the tutti-frutti ice cream and spread over the orange ice cream leaving a central hole. Pack the sorbet into this. Freeze until solid.

To transport, pack in an insulated freezer box or bag with several ice packs or dry ice. Before serving unmould the ice cream and peel away the polythene film. Serve in slices with wafers.

POACHED PEARS

SERVES 6-8

6-8 firm pears, such as Conference
1 lemon
1 orange
6 cloves
4 allspice berries
300ml/½ pint red wine
2 × 15ml spoons/2 tablespoons port
50g/2oz caster sugar
1 small cinnamon stick

Peel the pears but leave the stalks attached. Remove the cores from the base end using a small teaspoon. Pare the rind thinly from the lemon and orange and place in a pan with the pears. Add the juice from the fruit and cloves, allspice and wine. Bring the liquid to a very slow simmer and poach for 20 to 30 minutes until the pears are tender. Turn the pears occasionally so that they take up an even red colour. Remove the pears, rind and spices with a slotted spoon.

Allow the pears to cool.

Add the port, sugar and cinnamon to the pan and stir to dissolve the sugar. Bring to the boil and simmer until the syrup is thickened and reduced. Remove the cinnamon stick and cool the syrup.

Transport the pears in a sealed container with the syrup. Serve with single cream.

DARK AND WHITE CHOCOLATE MOUSSE

SERVES 4-6

Take great care when melting white chocolate – it very quickly turns into hard lumps if even slightly overheated. Grate the chocolate into a heatproof jug and stand it in a bowl of hot, not boiling, water. Stir until the chocolate has melted.

3 eggs, separated
3 × 15ml spoons/3 tablespoons caster sugar
100g/4oz plain chocolate, melted
75g/3oz white chocolate, very gently melted
2 × 15ml spoons/2 tablespoons Cointreau
150ml/¼ pint double cream, whipped

Whisk the egg yolks in a large bowl with the sugar until very thick and pale. Fold in the plain chocolate. In another bowl, whisk the egg whites until stiff. Mix together the white chocolate, Cointreau and cream and fold in the egg whites. Spoon the two mixtures alternately into small containers with lids and swirl the surface with a knife tip to give a marbled effect. Chill until set. Cover for transporting. Serve with wafers.

OLIVE AND ANCHOVY BREAD

MAKES 2 LOAVES

25g/1 öz fresh yeast
450ml/¾ pint hand hot water
25mg/½ vitamin C tablet, crushed (or ascorbic acid)
700g/1½lb strong plain flour
50g/2oz black olives, stoned and roughly chopped
50g/2oz green olives, stoned and roughly chopped
1 × 15ml spoon/1 tablespoon dried oregano
15g/½oz anchovies, drained and chopped

Blend the yeast, water and the vitamin C tablet together. Sift the flour into a warmed bowl. Stir in the olives, oregano and anchovies. Add the yeast liquid and mix to a dough. Knead on a floured surface until very soft, smooth and elastic. Shape the dough into two flat round loaves. Place on a greased baking sheet. Cover with oiled polythene film and allow to rise in a warm place until doubled in size (about 1 hour).

Remove the polythene film and sprinkle the loaves with a little more flour. Bake at 230°C/450°F/Gas 8 for 20 to 30 minutes until they sound hollow when tapped underneath and are golden-brown. Cool on a wire rack and serve broken into chunks.

ROSEMARY BREADSTICKS

MAKES 18

15g/½oz fresh yeast
250ml/8floz hand-hot water
25mg/½ tablet Vitamin C (or ascorbic acid), crushed
350g/12oz strong plain flour
1 × 5ml spoon/1 teaspoon salt
2 × 5ml spoons/2 teaspoons sugar
15g/½oz butter
1 × 5ml spoon/1 teaspoon fresh rosemary
2 × 15ml spoons/2 tablespoons olive oil
2 × 15ml spoons/2 tablespoons tomato purée
6 × 15ml spoons/6 tablespoons boiling water
1 × 5ml spoon/1 teaspoon ground rosemary

Blend the yeast and the hand-hot water. Stir in the crushed vitamin C tablet. Sift the flour, salt and sugar into a warmed bowl. Rub in the butter. Stir in the yeast liquid and rosemary. Mix to a soft dough then knead on a lightly floured surface for about 10 minutes. The dough should be smooth and elastic. Divide the dough into three pieces. Roll each out to a thin round the size of a dinner plate. Place each on a greased baking sheet. Cover with oiled polythene film and leave to rise in a warm place for about 50 minutes until doubled in size.

Brush the rounds with olive oil. Blend the tomato purée with the boiling water and stir in the ground rosemary. Spread this mixture over the breads. Slash the breads across deeply into wide fingers. Bake at 220°C/425°F/Gas 7 for 15 to 20 minutes until risen and golden underneath. Allow to cool on wire racks.

Transport the bread in paper bags and tear into fingers to serve.

VARIATION *Saffron Bread*
Make the basic dough as for Rosemary Bread-sticks but substitute 2 pinches of powdered saffron for the rosemary. Shape the dough into two round loaves. After proving, brush with milk and sprinkle with semolina. Slash the tops of the dough into diamond shapes and bake for 30 to 40 minutes. Break off large chunks to serve.

JAPONAISE FINGERS

MAKES 12

2 egg whites
100g/4oz caster sugar
100g/4oz ground almonds
FILLING
75g/3oz plain chocolate
1 × 5ml spoon/1 teaspoon coffee essence
85ml/3fl oz double cream

Whisk the egg whites until very stiff. Gradually sprinkle in two-thirds of the sugar while continuing to whisk, until the mixture is very stiff and glossy. Fold in the remaining sugar and almonds using a spatula. Spoon into a large piping bag fitted with a large plain nozzle and pipe 24 fingers on a greased and lined baking sheet. Bake at 170°C/325°F/Gas 3 for 45 minutes without browning. Cool on a wire rack.

To make the filling, place all the ingredients in a bowl and set over a pan of simmering water. Cook until melted and stir to blend. Cool. Whip the mixture until thick and fluffy and use to sandwich the fingers together in twos. Chill until set. Pack into a rigid container.

VARIATION   Japonaise Cakes
Make as for Japonaise Fingers but pipe the mixture into small flat rounds instead of fingers.

For the filling, cream together 100g/4oz butter, 175g/6oz sifted icing sugar and 2 × 5ml spoons/ 2 teaspoons coffee essence. Sandwich the rounds with a little filling and also pipe a small rosette of it on top of each cake. Finish each cake with a hazelnut on top.

FLORENTINES

MAKES 18

50g/2oz butter
50g/2oz caster sugar
50g/2oz blanched almonds, chopped
25g/1oz candied peel chopped
25g/1oz glacé cherries, chopped
1 × 15ml spoon/1 tablespoon cream
75g/3oz plain chocolate, melted

Place the butter and sugar in a small pan and heat gently until melted. Add the nuts, peel, cherries and cream. Drop small spoonfuls of the mixture, well spaced, on to baking trays lined with non-stick baking paper. Cook at 190°C/375°F/Gas 5 for 8 to 9 minutes. Leave to cool on the tray for 2 to 3 minutes then neaten the edges of the Florentines using a round pastry cutter. Lift from the paper with a palette knife and cool on a wire rack. When cool spread the flat sides of the Florentines with melted chocolate and mark in wavy lines with a fork. Leave to set.

Pack, interleaved with greaseproof paper, in a rigid container.

CHILDREN'S PICNICS

The novelty of eating out-of-doors – on the grass or perching on a rock – is half the fun of a picnic, and children appreciate this perhaps better than anyone. Almost any outdoor space is suitable, but best are those with plenty of room for games and adventures.

With no carpet to spill food on, nothing valuable to break and no party clothes to ruin, adults can relax while children run wild. The food can reflect this mood of excitement. Spiral-shaped Sausage Twirls, Tomato and Egg Butterflies and Eggy Footballs fit in with the party spirit. Bite-sized Barbecue Chicken Chunks, Mini Bacon Tarts and Cheesy Snack Biscuits are perfect for eating on the run. As the party winds down, a selection of brightly-coloured Cupcakes and cream-filled Chocolate Boxes provide a wonderful final surprise.

CHEESY SNACK BISCUITS

SERVES 8-10

225g/8oz plain flour
75g/3oz semolina
1 × 5ml spoon/1 teaspoon salt
pinch cayenne pepper
100g/4oz Cheddar cheese, very finely grated
225g/8oz butter
FILLING
100g/4oz cream cheese
6 × 15ml spoons/6 tablespoons natural yoghurt
2 × 15ml spoons/2 tablespoons smooth peanut
butter

Mix the flour, semolina, salt and pepper in a bowl. Stir in the cheese and rub in the butter until the mixture resembles fine breadcrumbs. Chill for 30 minutes. Knead the mixture with the hands to a firm dough. Roll out to 6mm/¼inch thick on a surface dusted with semolina. Cut out with small pastry cutters and transfer to a greased baking sheet. Bake at 180°C/350°F/Gas 4 for 25 minutes. Cool on a wire rack. To make the filling, cream together all the ingredients and use to sandwich the biscuits together.

Chill before packing into a rigid container.

BARBECUE CHICKEN CHUNKS

SERVES 6-8

2 × 15ml spoons/2 tablespoons thick honey
1 × 15ml spoon/1 tablespoon light brown sugar
1 × 15ml spoon/1 tablespoon white wine vinegar
1 × 15ml spoon/1 tablespoon tomato purée
150ml/¼ pint orange juice
1 × 15ml spoon/1 tablespoon soy sauce
1 × 5ml spoon/1 teaspoon Worcestershire sauce
pinch dry mustard powder
freshly-ground black pepper
3-4 chicken breasts, skinned, boned and cut into
chunks

Place the honey, sugar, vinegar, tomato purée, orange juice, sauces and mustard in a small pan. Bring to the boil and simmer for 10 minutes. The sauce should be of a syrupy consistency. Season with ground black pepper. Remove from the heat and stir the chicken pieces into the sauce. Remove them with tongs and set on a rack in a grill pan. Grill for 10 minutes, brushing with the remaining sauce and turning frequently.

Allow to cool and pack in a rigid container.

SAUSAGE TWIRLS

SERVES 6-8

225g/8 oz plain flour
100g/4 oz butter
1 × 5ml spoon/1 teaspoon mustard powder
large pinch salt
450g/1 lb chipolata sausages, cooked and cooled
beaten egg

Sift the flour into a bowl and rub in the butter. Stir in the mustard and salt. Add just enough water to bind to a firm dough (about 2½ × 15ml spoons/ 2½ tablespoons).

Wrap in polythene film and chill for 30 minutes. Roll out thinly on a lightly floured work surface and cut into long strips about 6mm/¼ in wide. Brush with beaten egg and roll the strips round the sausages in a spiral. Brush the pastry with beaten egg. Place on a greased baking sheet and bake at 200°C/400°F/Gas 6 for 10 to 15 minutes. Cool on a wire rack.

Pack in a rigid container.

SERVING SUGGESTION Pack 2 pots of mild mustard for dipping for those who want it.

CHEESE BAGELS

MAKES 12

15g/½ oz fresh yeast
300ml/½ pint hand hot water
450g/1 lb wholemeal flour
1½ × 5ml spoons/1½ teaspoons salt
25g/1 oz butter
100g/4 oz Cheddar cheese, grated
beaten egg
2 × 15ml spoons/2 tablespoons poppy seeds

Blend the yeast and water together. Mix the flour and salt together in a warmed bowl. Rub in the butter. Stir in the cheese. Pour in the yeast liquid and mix until the mixture leaves the sides of the bowl. Turn out the dough onto a floured work surface. Knead for about 10 minutes until very smooth, soft and elastic. Divide the dough into 12 pieces and shape each into small flat rounds. Make a hole in the centre of each to form rings. Poach the rings in a large pan of simmering water for about 20 seconds until they start to puff up. Remove them with a slotted spoon and place on greased baking sheets. Cover with oiled polythene film and allow to rise in a warm place for 1 hour. Brush with beaten egg and sprinkle with poppy seeds. Bake at 230°C/450°F/Gas 8 for 10 to 15 minutes. Cool on a wire rack. Split and butter before packing.

SAVOURY TOMATO BUTTERFLIES

MAKES 16

225g/8oz puff pastry
1 egg yolk
1 × 15ml spoon/1 tablespoon tomato purée
1 × 5ml spoon/1 teaspoon yeast extract

Roll out the pastry to a rectangle 30 × 20cm/12 × 8 inches. Cut into strips 20 × 7.5cm/8 × 3 inches. Beat together the egg yolk, tomato purée and yeast extract. Brush down the centre of three of the strips. Place the strips on top of each other, with the egg yolk upwards, matching the edges to form a neat stack. Lay the unbrushed strip on top. Press the stack down the centre with a rolling pin to seal them together. Cut the stack across into 16 slices 1 × 7.5cm/½ × 3 inches. Place the slices on a greased baking sheet and fan out the ends. Bake at 220°C/425°F/Gas 7 for 15 minutes. Cool on a wire rack before packing into a rigid container.

EGGY FOOTBALLS

SERVES 8-10

150ml/¼ pint water
50g/2oz butter
65g/2½ oz strong plain flour
pinch dry mustard powder
2 eggs, beaten
2 × 15ml spoons/2 tablespoons Parmesan cheese, grated
FILLING
3 hard-boiled eggs, shelled, mashed
25g/1oz butter, melted
2 × 15ml spoons/2 tablespoons mayonnaise
1 × 15ml spoon/1 tablespoon fresh parsley, chopped

Place the water and butter in a small pan and heat until the butter melts. Bring to the boil and add the flour. Beat for 1 minute over the heat, to a smooth mixture. Stir in the mustard. Allow to cool slightly. Gradually beat in just sufficient eggs to make a smooth, glossy paste that just holds its shape. Spoon into a piping bag fitted with a large plain nozzle. Pipe small rounds onto greased baking sheets and sprinkle each with a little Parmesan cheese.

Bake at 220°C/425°F/Gas 7 for 20 to 25 minutes until crisp and browned. Cool on a wire rack.

To make the filling, mix the ingredients together and check the seasoning. Chill.

Just before packing, split the buns and fill each with a little of the mixture.

MINI BACON TARTS

MAKES 12

100g/4oz plain flour
100g/4oz self-raising wholemeal flour
100g/4oz butter
pinch of salt
8 × 15ml spoons/8 tablespoons iced water
(approximately)
FILLING
1 × 15ml spoon/1 tablespoon oil
6 rashers streaky bacon, without rinds, chopped
1 onion, peeled and chopped
100g/4oz Double Gloucester cheese, diced
150ml/¼ pint double cream
4 × 15ml spoons/4 tablespoons milk
2 eggs
freshly-ground white pepper
50g/2oz sweetcorn kernels

Place the flours in a bowl and rub in the butter. Stir in the salt and enough water to bind to a firm dough. Knead lightly and roll out on a floured work surface. Cut out rounds with a pastry cutter and use to line the cups in a bun tin.

To make the filling, heat the oil in a pan and fry the bacon and onion together for 4 minutes. Drain and place in the bowl of a food processor with the cheese, cream, milk and eggs. Add salt and freshly-ground white pepper. Work for a few seconds to finely chop and mix the ingredients. Stir in the sweetcorn and divide the mixture between the pastry cups.

Bake at 190°C/375°F/Gas 5 for 20 to 25 minutes until set and golden-brown. Cool on a wire rack.

Pack in a rigid container layered with grease-proof paper.

SESAME PUFF FINGERS

SERVES 8-10

350g/12oz puff pastry
1 × 15ml spoon/1 tablespoon yeast extract
1 × 15ml spoon/1 tablespoon boiling water
2 × 15ml spoons/2 tablespoons sesame seeds

Roll out the pastry thinly on a floured surface to a large rectangle. Blend the yeast extract with the water and brush all over the surface of the pastry. Sprinkle with the seeds and press them on. Cut into strips about 13 × 1cm/5 × ½ inch. Twist each strip several times from both ends and lay on baking sheets. Bake at 190°C/375°F/Gas 6 for 10 minutes until golden-brown and crisp. Cool on a wire rack and pack into rigid containers for transporting.

EGG AND WATERCRESS MINI LOAVES

MAKES 8

8 miniature brown loaves
salt, pepper
4 hard-boiled eggs
3 × 15ml spoons/3 tablespoons mayonnaise
⅓ bunch watercress, trimmed and chopped
pinch paprika pepper
1 × 5ml spoon/1 teaspoon lemon juice

Cut a slice from the top of each of the mini loaves and reserve. Scoop out the crumb from inside the loaves with a pointed teaspoon. Season inside the loaves with salt and pepper. Chop the eggs roughly and mix with mayonnaise, watercress, pepper and lemon juice. Pile into the loaves and replace the tops. Pack in a rigid container and chill before transporting.

CHEESE, FRUIT AND NUT NIBBLES

SERVES 6-8

4 red-skinned apples, cored, cut into dice
2 green-skinned apples, cored, cut into dice
2 × 15ml spoons/2 tablespoons lemon juice
50g/2oz sultanas
50g/2oz shelled peanuts
225g/8oz Cheddar cheese, cut into dice

Place the apples and lemon juice in a container and mix so that the apples are coated in juice. Add the sultanas, nuts and cheese. Chill. Seal the container for transporting.

HERBY SAUSAGES AND MUSTARD DIP

SERVES 6-8

450g/1 lb oz herby cocktail sausages
DIP
4 × 15ml spoons/4 tablespoons mayonnaise
4 × 15ml spoons/4 tablespoons thick Greek yoghurt
1-2 × 15ml spoons/1-2 tablespoons mild American
burger mustard
2 × 15ml spoons/2 tablespoons tomato sauce
1 × 15ml spoon/1 tablespoon onion, finely chopped
1 × 15ml spoon/1 tablespoon fresh parsley, chopped

Place the sausages in a roasting tin and bake at 200°C/400°F/Gas 6 for about 20 minutes. Drain them thoroughly on absorbent kitchen paper. Cool and pack into a rigid container with cocktail sticks for spearing.

For the dip, blend all the ingredients and pack into a small sealed container.

CHEESE AND CELERY NUT BREAD

MAKES 1 LOAF

225g/8 oz self-raising flour, sifted
pinch dry mustard powder
50g/2 oz butter
100g/4 oz Cheddar cheese, grated
75g/3 oz celery, finely chopped
75g/3 oz walnuts, coarsely chopped
1 × 15ml spoon/1 tablespoon oil
½ onion peeled and chopped
3 rashers streaky bacon, without rinds and chopped
2 × 15ml spoons/2 tablespoons fresh parsley,
chopped
1 egg, beaten
150ml/¼ pint milk

Place the flour and mustard in a bowl. Rub in the butter and stir in the cheese, celery and nuts. Heat the oil in a pan and fry the onion and bacon for 3 minutes. Drain and cool. Add to the flour. Beat the parsley, egg and milk together. Stir into the flour mixture and mix to a soft dough. Turn into a greased and lined 900g/2 lb loaf tin and smooth the top. Bake at 190°C/375°F/Gas 5 for 1 hour until risen and golden. Cool in the tin for 20 minutes. Turn out on to a wire rack.

Slice and butter before packing.

SERVING SUGGESTION Cheese and celery nut bread could also be eaten with cheese and slices of ham, with crisp lettuce leaves.

STRAWBERRY CUPCAKES

MAKES 12

100g/4 oz butter
100g/4 oz caster sugar
2 eggs, beaten
100g/4 oz self-raising flour
few drops pink food colouring
TOPPING
75g/3 oz white chocolate, very gently melted (see
page 41)
25g/1 oz butter
50g/2 oz icing sugar
few drops red colouring
boiling water

Cream together the butter and sugar until light
and fluffy. Gradually beat in the eggs and finally
fold in the flour and enough food colouring to
make the mixture dark pink. (The colouring fades
when baked so add a little more than you think
necessary.) Divide between 12 paper cases set in
bun tins. Knock the tin on the work surface to
distribute the mixture evenly. Bake at 180°C/350°F/
Gas 4 for 10 to 15 minutes until golden-brown.
Remove from the oven and cool on a wire rack.

To make the topping, blend the chocolate and
butter and smooth over the cakes to make a flat
surface inside the paper cases. Blend the icing
sugar with a few drops of colouring and boiling
water to make a thick consistency. Pipe thin
parallel lines of the icing over the chocolate. Draw
the end of a skewer backwards and forwards
through the icing to create a feathered pattern.
Allow to set in a cool place. Pack the cakes in a
rigid container in one layer.

VARIATION   *Lemon Cupcakes*
Make as for the Strawberry Cupcakes but use the
finely grated rind of 1 lemon instead of colouring
in the cake. For the icing, use lemon juice in place
of water and colour it with a few drops of yellow
colouring.

CHOCOLATE BOXES

MAKES 9

350g/12 oz plain or milk chocolate, melted
15cm/6 in-square slab plain sponge cake
apricot jam, warmed and sieved
150ml/¼ pint whipping cream, whipped
DECORATION
miniature marzipan fruits

Spread the chocolate out thinly over a large sheet
of non-stick baking paper or waxed paper. Leave to
set in a cool dry place. Cut the sponge cake into
9 smaller squares. Cut the set chocolate into
squares to fit the sides and tops of the cake
squares. Spread the sides of the sponge cakes with
jam. Remove the chocolate squares from the
paper and press them onto the sides of the cake
squares. Pipe or pile whipped cream on top of the
cake squares, add a marzipan fruit and set a final
chocolate square at an angle on the cream as the
lid. Chill well. Pack closely in one layer in a rigid
container and keep cool.

CARAMEL FINGERS

MAKES 14

225g/8oz butter
175g/6oz plain flour
175g/6oz caster sugar
200g/7oz tin sweetened condensed milk
1½ × 15ml spoons/1½ tablespoons golden syrup
175g/6oz plain chocolate, melted

Rub half the butter into the flour until the mixture resembles breadcrumbs. Stir in 50g/2oz of the sugar. Knead the mixture with the hands until it comes together to form a smooth dough. Press it evenly into a greased 18 × 28cm/7 × 11 inch swiss roll tin. Bake at 180°C/350°F/Gas 4 for 20 minutes until golden. Cool in the tin.

Place the remaining butter, sugar, milk and syrup in a pan. Heat gently then bring to the boil for about 5 minutes, stirring continuously. The sugar will caramelise and the mixture should turn a pale brown. Remove from the heat and beat for 2 to 3 minutes. Pour onto the shortbread in the tin and leave to cool and set. Spread the melted chocolate over the surface and mark with a fork. Mark into fingers and allow to set. Cut into bars.

Transport in the tin layered in waxed kitchen paper and keep as cool as possible.

LIME AND STRAWBERRY JELLY MOUSSE

SERVES 8-10

1 packet lime jelly
1 packet strawberry jelly
425g/14oz tin evaporated milk, chilled overnight
DECORATION
hundreds and thousands

Make up the jellies as directed on the pack but add only enough water to make 450ml/¾ pint. Allow the jellies to cool. In a clean, cool bowl, whisk the evaporated milk until it becomes very thick and frothy. Divide it into two portions. Just as the jellies are beginning to thicken, whisk each into a portion of evaporated milk. Quickly spoon the mixtures alternately into clear plastic drinking tumblers. Swirl the desserts with the end of a wooden spoon to marble the colours together. Chill until completely set.

Sprinkle the top with hundreds and thousands just before serving.

LEMON MERINGUE ICE CREAM

SERVES 6-8

150ml/¼ pint water
150g/5 oz caster sugar
3 eggs, separated
150ml/¼ pint double cream, whipped
2 meringue nests, roughly crushed
4 digestive biscuits, roughly crushed
1 lemon, grated rind and juice
6-8 crisp wafer cones

Place the water and sugar in a small pan and heat gently, stirring until the sugar has dissolved. Bring to the boil, without stirring and boil to 110°C/225°F. Whisk the egg yolks until pale and thick and then gradually whisk in the hot syrup, pouring it in a thin stream. Continue to whisk until the mixture has cooled and thickened. Fold in the whipped cream, meringue, biscuits and lemon rind and juice. Finally whisk the egg whites until stiff and fold in. Pour into a shallow freezer container and freeze until solid. Spoon the ice cream into crisp wafer cones and re-freeze.

Transport the cones in insulated freezer bags or boxes, packed with ice packs.

FRESH LEMON AND LIME SQUASH

SERVES 6-8

3 lemons
3 limes
350g/12 oz sugar
200ml/7 fl oz water

Scrub the fruit in hot water. Grate the rinds finely and squeeze the juice. Place the rind and sugar in a pan. Add the water and heat gently, stirring, until the sugar has dissolved. Bring to the boil and cook for 2 minutes. Allow to cool and stir in the fruit juice. Strain and chill. Transport in a sealed bottle and dilute with iced water or mineral water to serve.

FOOD FOR LOVE

A well-planned picnic can be one of the most romantic ways of celebrating for two. Tempting delicacies can be prepared in advance, leaving plenty of time to talk and relax.

Choose light, attractive dishes which reflect the romance of the occasion. The combination of shrimps, mace, root ginger, lemon juice, Tabasco sauce and chives makes Spicy Potted Shrimps a memorable appetizer. Follow, perhaps, with Chicken Tikka Pieces which come skewered like a kebab and garnished with lemon wedges to make a spectacular display. Cut the Crab and Chicken Roll into spiral-shaped slices and serve with a light salad as an alternative.

The Orange and Rosewater Bavarois, decorated with sugared rose petals, makes an appropriately dreamy dessert. Then, for a final touch of elegance, present a pretty dish full of Fondant Dipped Fruits.

SALMON AND CREAM CHEESE MOUSSE ·

SERVES 2

200g/7 oz tin salmon, drained
300ml/½ pint liquid aspic
100g/4 oz cream cheese, softened
1 hard-boiled egg, chopped
1 lemon, grated rind and juice
2 × 15ml spoons/2 tablespoons mayonnaise
2 × 15ml spoons/2 tablespoons fresh parsley,
chopped
few drops Tabasco sauce
salt, pepper
GARNISH
fresh prawns

Place the salmon and aspic in a food processor or blender and work until smooth. Stir in the cream cheese and the remaining ingredients.

Season and pour into an oiled fish-shaped mould. Chill until set.

Transport in the mould and turn out just before serving. Garnish with prawns.

SPICY POTTED SHRIMPS

APPETIZER   SERVES 2

175g/6 oz peeled shrimps
pinch ground mace
½ × 5ml spoon/½ teaspoon root ginger, freshly
grated
few drops lemon juice
few drops Tabasco sauce
1 × 15ml spoon/1 tablespoon fresh chives, chopped
175g/6 oz butter, melted
freshly-ground white pepper

Mix together the shrimps, mace, ginger, lemon juice, Tabasco and chives. Put 50g/2 oz of the butter in a pan and add the shrimp mixture. Stir over a very gentle heat until the butter is absorbed. Season with freshly-ground white pepper. Spoon the mixture into two ramekin dishes and smooth down. Strain the remaining butter through scalded muslin and pour over the surface of each ramekin to seal. Chill overnight.

Transport in the ramekins.

SERVING SUGGESTION   Serve with thinly sliced brown bread.

MANGO SOUFFLÉS

SERVES 2

2 eggs, separated
50g/2oz caster sugar
1 mango, peeled, stone removed and puréed
15g/½oz gelatine, dissolved in 3 × 15ml spoons/
3 tablespoons boiling water, cooled
½ lemon, finely grated rind and juice
150ml/¼ pint double cream
DECORATION
slices of lemon

Whisk the egg yolks and sugar together until very pale and thick. Stir in the mango purée, cooled gelatine, lemon juice and rind. Whip the cream until thick and fold in. Finally whisk the egg whites until stiff and fold in. Pour into individual dishes for transportation and chill until set. Decorate with lemon slices.

CHEESE, CHIVES AND NUT PARCELS

MAKES 6

175g/6oz cream cheese, softened
2 × 15ml spoons/2 tablespoons fresh chives, snipped
50g/2oz pistachio nuts, chopped
½ × 5ml spoon/½ teaspoon paprika pepper
6 sheets filo pastry
3 × 15ml spoons/3 tablespoons olive oil

Blend the cream cheese with the chives, nuts and pepper. Brush a sheet of filo pastry all over with olive oil. Place a spoonful of filling at one end of the pastry and fold and roll the pastry round the filling to make a neat sausage-shaped parcel. Place on a baking sheet. Repeat with the remaining pastry and filling. Brush the parcels again with oil and bake at 200°C/400°F/Gas 6 for 10 to 15 minutes until golden-brown and crisp. Cool on a wire rack.

Transport in a rigid container.

CHICKEN TIKKA PIECES

MAIN DISH   SERVES 2

2 chicken breasts, skinned, boned and cut into
chunks
MARINADE
150ml/¼ pint natural yoghurt
pinch chilli powder
¼ × 5ml spoon/¼ teaspoon ground ginger
¼ × 5ml spoon/¼ teaspoon turmeric
½ × 5ml spoon/½ teaspoon coriander seeds, freshly
ground
½ × 5ml spoon/½ teaspoon garlic purée
freshly-ground black pepper
1 × 15ml spoon/1 tablespoon lemon juice
GARNISH
lemon wedges

Place the chicken pieces in a bowl. Mix together
the yoghurt, spices, garlic and lemon juice. Season
with salt and freshly-ground black pepper. Pour
over the chicken and mix well. Cover and marinate
overnight in the refrigerator. On the following day,
thread the chicken pieces onto two metal skewers
and brush with the remaining marinade. Grill for 7
minutes on each side. Cool and pack the skewers
in a rigid container with lemon wedges for garnish.

CRAB AND CHICKEN ROLL

MAIN DISH   SERVES 2

40g/1½oz butter
25g/1oz plain flour
150ml/¼ pint milk
3 eggs, separated
FILLING
225g/8oz cooked chicken
225g/8oz crabmeat
4 × 15ml spoons/4 tablespoons mayonnaise
1 × 5ml spoon/1 teaspoon paprika pepper
¼ × 5ml spoon/¼ teaspoon cayenne pepper
1 lemon, finely grated rind and juice

Melt the butter in a small pan and stir in the flour.
Cook for 1 minute. Gradually blend in the milk
until a smooth sauce is formed. Remove from the
heat and beat in the egg yolks. Whisk the egg
whites until stiff and gently fold into the sauce
mixture. Spread evenly into a greased and lined
23 × 33cm/9 × 13inch swiss roll tin. Bake at
190°C/375°F/Gas 5 for 15 to 20 minutes until risen
and golden-brown. Turn out onto non-stick baking
paper and trim the crispy edges. Roll up with the
paper inside. Allow to cool.

To make the filling, blend all the ingredients
together and season with freshly-ground black
pepper. Unroll the cooked roll and remove the
paper. Spread the roll with the filling and roll up
once more. Cover and chill.

Slice and pack in a rigid container with the
slices interleaved with greaseproof paper.

SERVING SUGGESTION   Serve sliced as an appetizer or for a more substantial meal, with a salad,
such as Watercress and Palm Heart (page 74).

CUCUMBER, MUSHROOM AND STRAWBERRY SALAD *

SERVES 2-4

¼ cucumber, peeled
50g/2oz button mushrooms, sliced
DRESSING
100g/4oz strawberries, hulled and puréed
2 × 15ml spoons/2 tablespoons oil
1 × 5ml spoon/1 teaspoon lemon juice
6 mint leaves, shredded

Slice the cucumber in half lengthways and remove the seeds with the point of a teaspoon. Slice thickly and mix with the mushrooms. Chill. Transport in a small container.

To make the dressing, mix all the ingredients together and transport separately. Pour over salad just before serving.

BULGAR WHEAT SALAD

SERVES 2-4

100g/4oz bulgar wheat, (burghul wheat)
2 spring onions, trimmed and sliced
75g/3oz peeled prawns
1 lemon, grated rind only
3 × 15ml spoons/3 tablespoons fresh parsley, chopped
pinch of cumin powder
2 × 15ml spoons/2 tablespoons french dressing

Place the bulgar wheat in a large bowl and cover with lukewarm water for 10 minutes. Squeeze the water out of the wheat and dry it on kitchen paper. Mix in the remaining ingredients and season with plenty of freshly ground black pepper. Chill before serving.

GINGERED PEARS WITH CARAMEL

SERVES 2

2 firm pears, peeled with stalks left intact
50g/2 oz demerara sugar
150ml/¼ pint water
150ml/¼ pint white wine
1 orange, grated rind and juice
2 pieces stem ginger, sliced
3 × 15ml spoons/3 tablespoons stem ginger syrup
1 cinnamon stick

Remove the base and cores from the pears with a small teaspoon. Place the remaining ingredients in a pan and heat gently, stirring, until the sugar dissolves. Add the pears and poach gently for 15 to 20 minutes until tender. Remove the pears to a container. Bring the contents of the saucepan to a rapid boil for 5 to 10 minutes until syrupy. Remove the cinnamon stick and pour the syrup over the pears. Chill before serving with single cream.

ORANGE AND ROSEWATER BAVAROIS

SERVES 2

2 egg yolks
50g/2 oz icing sugar
150ml/¼ pint milk, scalded
few drops rosewater
10g/¼ oz gelatine
1 × 15ml spoon/1 tablespoon boiling water
1 orange, finely grated rind and juice
150ml/¼ pint whipping cream, whipped
DECORATION
rose petals
egg white
caster sugar

Whisk the egg yolks and sugar in a large bowl until thick and pale. Gradually whisk in the milk. Set the bowl over a pan of simmering water and cook, stirring, until the custard is thick enough to coat the back of a wooden spoon. Remove from the heat. Stir in the rosewater. Dissolve the gelatine in the boiling water and add to the custard with the orange rind and juice. Cover the surface with polythene film to prevent a skin forming and allow to cool.

Fold the whipped cream into the custard and pour into two small, oiled moulds or serving dishes. Chill until set. Transport the bavaroise in the moulds.

To make the decoration, paint both sides of rose petals with egg white using a small paint brush. Dredge thickly with caster sugar and shake off the excess. Leave to dry on absorbent kitchen paper. Pack carefully in a rigid container padded with kitchen paper.

Just before serving, ease the set bavarois away from the mould sides with the fingertips and turn out. Decorate with the sugared rose petals.

SPONGE DROPS

MAKES 10

2 eggs
50g/2 oz caster sugar
50g/2 oz plain flour
few drops vanilla essence
caster sugar for dredging

Place the eggs and sugar in a large bowl and whisk them until they become very thick and foamy. Sift the flour twice and fold into the mixture with a few drops of vanilla essence. Spoon the mixture into a piping bag fitted with a large plain nozzle and quickly pipe small rounds onto baking sheets lined with greaseproof paper. Dredge the rounds heavily with caster sugar and very quickly tilt the paper sideways to remove the excess sugar. Bake the drops at 200°C/400°F/Gas 6 for 10 to 12 minutes to a pale golden colour. Cool on a wire rack.

Pack in a rigid container lined with absorbent kitchen paper.

VARIATION *Sponge Fingers*
Make as for Sponge Drops but pipe the mixture into fingers instead of rounds. After baking, dip the ends in melted chocolate and allow to set on a wire rack. Pack in a rigid container lined with waxed paper.

FONDANT DIPPED FRUITS

SERVES 2-4

FONDANT ICING
100g/4 oz granulated sugar
25ml/1 fl oz water
¼ × 5ml spoon/¼ teaspoon liquid glucose, or good pinch cream of tartar
175g/6 oz fresh fruits such as cherries, strawberries and grapes, with hulls, stalks etc. if possible

To make the fondant icing, dissolve the sugar in water over gentle heat. Bring to the boil and add the glucose, (or the cream of tartar). Boil to 130°C/250°F on a sugar thermometer (soft ball stage). Remove from the heat to cool a little, then pour the syrup onto a wetted work surface. Leave for 1 to 2 minutes then, using a wooden spatula, work the syrup from the outside edges to the centre until the fondant forms. Knead small pieces in the fingers until smooth. Form a ball and leave to 'mellow' for 1 hour.

Next, place the fondant in a bowl over simmering water. Stir, then add sufficient water to thin the fondant to the consistency of thick cream.

Dip the fruit into the fondant to coat the bottom half. Place on non-stick baking paper or waxed paper to dry. Pack the fruit carefully, at the last moment, layered with greaseproof paper into a rigid container.

STRAWBERRY AND GOOSEBERRY FOOLS

SERVES 2-4

100g/4oz gooseberries
50g/2oz caster sugar
2 egg yolks
25g/1oz icing sugar
300ml/½ pint creamy milk
150ml/¼ pint double cream, whipped
175g/6oz strawberries, hulled and puréed
DECORATION
fresh sliced strawberries

Place the gooseberries, caster sugar and 1 × 15ml spoon/1 tablespoon of water in a small, tightly-lidded pan. Set over a gentle heat and cook for 5 to 8 minutes until the gooseberries are very tender. Press the mixture through a sieve and cool. Place the egg yolks and icing sugar in a large bowl and whisk until very thick. Set the bowl over a pan of simmering water and whisk in the milk. Cook gently until the custard is thick enough to coat the back of a wooden spoon. Press a sheet of polythene film over the surface of the custard and leave to cool. When cold, stir in the gooseberry purée and the cream. Pour into small dishes, swirling the strawberry purée as you pour. Chill before serving, decorated with strawberries.

CREAMY DUTCH SYLLABUB

SERVES 2-3

150ml/¼ pint single cream
150ml/¼ pint double cream
150ml/¼ pint thick Greek yoghurt
2 × 15ml spoons/2 tablespoons stem ginger, chopped
2 × 15ml spoons/2 tablespoons stem ginger syrup
2 × 15ml spoons/2 tablespoons advocaat liqueur
1 orange, finely grated rind only

Mix the single and double cream and whisk until stiff. Fold in the yoghurt. Blend the stem ginger, syrup, liqueur and orange rind. Stir into the cream. Spoon into containers and chill well before the journey. Serve with sponge drops.

MARZIPAN TARTLETS

SERVES 2

100g/4 oz shortcrust pastry
2 × 15ml spoons/2 tablespoons raspberry conserve
FILLING
15g/½ oz ground almonds
40g/1½ oz marzipan, grated
50g/2 oz butter
50g/2 oz caster sugar
1 egg, beaten
25g/1 oz self-raising flour
DECORATION
50g/2 oz icing sugar, sifted
1-2 × 5 ml spoons/1-2 teaspoons lemon juice

Line 2 10cm/4 inch-diameter tartlet tins with the pastry. Spread the conserve evenly on the base of the pastry tartlets. To make the filling, mix the ground almonds and the marzipan together. Beat the butter with the caster sugar until very light and fluffy. Gradually beat in the egg and finally fold in the almond mixture and the flour. Divide between the pastry cases and smooth the tops. Bake at 190°C/375°F/Gas 5 for 20 to 25 minutes until risen and firm. As the tartlets cool in their tins blend the icing sugar and just enough lemon juice to make a thin cream. Spread over the tarts and leave to cool. Transport in the tins.

HERBED FRENCH STICK

MAKES 1 LOAF

15g/½ oz fresh yeast
250ml/8 fl oz hand-hot milk
25mg/½ tablet vitamin C, crushed
350/12 oz strong plain flour
1 × 5ml spoon/1 teaspoon salt
2 × 5ml spoons/2 teaspoons sugar
25g/1 oz butter
1 × 15ml spoon/1 tablespoon fresh parsley, chopped
1 × 15ml spoon/1 tablespoon fresh rosemary, chopped
1 × 5ml spoon/1 teaspoon fresh thyme, chopped
beaten egg
2 × 15ml spoons/2 tablespoons sesame seeds

Blend the yeast and water and stir in the crushed vitamin C tablet. Mix the flour, salt and sugar in a warmed bowl. Rub in the butter and stir in the herbs. Pour in the yeast liquid and mix to a soft dough. Knead on a lightly floured surface for 10 minutes until soft, smooth and elastic. Shape the dough into a long French stick and place on a greased baking sheet. Cover with oiled polythene film and leave to rise in a warm place for about 1 hour until doubled in size. Remove the film, brush with beaten egg and sprinkle with seeds. Bake at 230°C/450°F/Gas 8 for 15 to 20 minutes until golden-brown and sounds hollow when tapped underneath. Cool on a wire rack.

Just before serving break the loaf into pieces and serve with garlic butter.

Garlic butter Cream 100g/4 oz butter with 1 × 15ml spoon/1 tablespoon garlic purée and 1 × 15ml spoon/1 tablespoon chopped fresh parsley. Form into a neat pat and wrap in foil. Chill before transporting.

EXTRAVAGANT
ENTERTAINING

Some picnic occasions call for a more formal approach than others. A day at the races, a school speech day or an elegant garden party are good excuses for a luxuriously sophisticated spread.

Choose dishes to convey the glamour of the event. Pork Satay makes an exotic appetizer or, alternatively, Mushroom-stuffed Brioches and Savoury Stilton Mille Feuilles are tempting with their freshly-baked pastry and delicious fillings.

For the main course, Chicken Galantine, served with a selection of salads, looks and tastes impressive. Choose from Celery, Ham and Carrot Salad, Cold Parslied Ratatouille Salad and Watercress and Palm Heart Salad for a tasteful combination.

For a final touch, present a spectacular dessert. Both the Special Summer Pudding and the Coeur à la Crème (a heart-shaped dessert served with fresh strawberries or raspberries) would make appropriately flamboyant conclusions.

PORK SATAY

APPETIZER   SERVES 4

225g/8 oz pork fillet
25g/1 oz butter
SAUCE
1 × 15ml spoon/1 tablespoon oil
½ onion, peeled and chopped
25g/1 oz creamed coconut
120ml/4 fl oz boiling water
pinch chilli powder
¼ × 5ml spoon/¼ teaspoon turmeric
¼ × 5ml spoon/¼ teaspoon *garam marsala*
2 × 15ml spoons/2 tablespoons crunchy peanut
butter
1 × 15ml spoon/1 tablespoon fresh lime juice
freshly-ground black pepper
GARNISH
¼ red pepper, cut into shreds
1 × 15ml spoon/1 tablespoon shredded coconut

Fry the pork fillet in the butter over a moderate heat for about 20 minutes, turning frequently. Drain and cool. Put aside.

Heat the oil and fry the onion until soft. Dissolve the creamed coconut in the boiling water and pour into the onion. Stir in the spices, peanut butter and lime juice. Season with freshly-ground black pepper. Cool. Pack into a sealed container.

Slice the pork into small pieces. Pack in a rigid container garnished with the pepper and coconut. Supply wooden cocktail sticks for spearing the pork to dip in the sauce.

MUSHROOM BRIOCHES

APPETIZER   MAKES 12

15g/½ oz fresh yeast
3 × 15ml spoons/3 tablespoons warm water
1 × 5ml spoon/1 teaspoon sugar
250g/9 oz strong plain flour, sifted
50g/2 oz butter
2 eggs, beaten
FILLING
350g/12 oz flat mushrooms, chopped
75g/3 oz butter
few drops Tabasco sauce
120ml/4 fl oz white wine
100g/4 oz cream cheese
freshly-ground black pepper
beaten egg, to glaze

Blend the yeast with the water. Blend in the sugar and 2 × 15ml spoons/2 tablespoons of the flour. Cover and leave in a warm place for about 20 minutes until frothy. Mix the remaining flour and salt in a warmed bowl. Rub in the butter. Whisk the eggs into the yeast batter and pour into the flour. Work to a soft dough. Knead until smooth and elastic. Place in an oiled polythene bag and leave in a warm place until doubled in size.

To make the filling, cook the mushrooms in the butter, Tabasco sauce and wine for 6 minutes. Boil rapidly until the juices are reduced to 2 × 15ml spoons/2 tablespoons. Stir in the cream cheese and season with black pepper. Cool.

Knock back the risen brioche dough and divide it into 12 equal pieces. Grease 12 brioche tins.

Cut a quarter off one piece of dough. Flatten the remaining dough into a circle. Place 1 × 15ml spoon/1 tablespoon of filling in the centre and bring the dough up to completely enclose the filling. Form into a ball. Place in a prepared tin. Form the small piece of dough into a ball and press into the centre of the brioche in the tin. Repeat with the remaining 11 pieces of dough and filling. Place the brioche tins on a baking sheet and cover with oiled polythene film. Leave in a warm place to prove (about 30 minutes) until puffy. Brush each with beaten egg and bake at 220°C/425°F/Mark 7 for 15 to 20 minutes until golden-brown. Remove from the tins and cool on a wire rack. Pack in a rigid container.

SAVOURY STILTON MILLE FEUILLES

APPETIZER   SERVES 6-8

350g/12 oz puff pastry
FILLING
225g/8 oz skimmed milk cheese
3 × 15ml spoons/3 tablespoons mayonnaise
100g/4 oz Stilton cheese, rind removed
2 × 15ml spoons/2 tablespoons fresh chives,
chopped
GARNISH
walnuts, chopped

Roll the pastry out on a floured surface to 6mm/ ¼ inch thick and cut into three large rectangles. Place on wetted baking sheets and chill for 15 minutes. Prick all over with a fork and bake at 220°C/425°F/Mark 7 for 15 to 20 minutes until risen and golden. Trim the edges neatly and cool on a wire rack.

To make the filling, soften the skimmed milk cheese in a bowl with the mayonnaise. Crumble in the Stilton and stir into the mixture with the chives. Season with freshly-ground black pepper. Spread each of the pastry rectangles with one-third of the mixture. Layer up the pastry pieces into a neat stack. Sprinkle the top with chopped walnuts and chill.

Cut into slices before packing between sheets of greaseproof paper in a rigid container.

SERVING SUGGESTION The cheese-filled pastries would complement a Ratatouille Salad (page 72).

CRAB AND ALMOND QUICHE

SERVES 4-6

PASTRY
50g/2 oz butter
100g/4 oz plain flour
1 × 5ml spoon/1 teaspoon paprika pepper
1 × 5ml spoon/1 teaspoon wholegrain mustard
powder
2-3 × 15ml spoons/2-3 tablespoons iced water
FILLING
3 eggs, beaten
250ml/8 fl oz single cream
2 spring onions, trimmed and sliced
200g/7 oz tin white crabmeat, drained
1 × 15ml spoon/1 tablespoon tomato purée
1 × 5ml spoon/1 teaspoon paprika pepper
few drops Tabasco sauce
pinch of chilli powder
25g/1 oz flaked almonds, toasted

To make the pastry rub the butter into the flour. Stir in the pepper and mustard and just enough water to make a firm dough. Wrap in polythene film and chill for 20 minutes. Roll out the pastry thinly and use to line a 20cm/8 inch flan tin or dish.

To make the filling, whisk together the eggs and cream. Stir in the spring onions, crabmeat and remaining ingredients. Pour gently into the pastry case and bake at 180°C/350°F/Gas 4 for 25 to 30 minutes. Cool and transport in the tin or dish. Cut into slices to serve.

CHICKEN AND SPINACH ROLLS

SERVES 6

6 chicken breasts, skinned and boned
100g/4oz frozen chopped spinach, thawed and
drained to remove excess liquid
1×15ml spoon/1 tablespoon egg white
1×5ml spoon/1teaspoon ground nutmeg
pinch of cumin powder
2 × 15ml spoons/2 tablespoons pistachio nuts, finely
chopped
150ml/¼ pint white wine
SAUCE
300ml/½ pint thick Greek yoghurt
1 lemon, grated rind and juice
GARNISH
lambs lettuce

Carefully remove the loose fillet from the under-side of each chicken breast and reserve. Place the breasts between sheets of polythene film and beat with a rolling pin until flattened to about 6mm/¼ inch thick. Remove the film. Place the reserved fillets in a food processor with the spinach, egg white, nutmeg, cumin and nuts. Blend until smooth. Divide the filling between the breasts and spread it evenly over each. Roll up the chicken to make neat shapes and place on a piece of foil. Sprinkle with wine and plenty of freshly-ground black pepper. Seal the parcels.

Bake at 180°C/350°F/Gas 4 for 25 minutes. Allow to cool in the foil. Remove to a rigid container for transportation. Mix the sauce ingredients and transport separately.

SERVING SUGGESTION Serve the chicken in slices garnished with lambs lettuce.

GARLIC AND HAZELNUT ROAST TURKEY

SERVES 8-10

5.5kg/12lb oven-ready turkey
salt, pepper
1 onion, finely chopped
1-2 cloves garlic, crushed
1 lemon, finely grated rind and juice
2 × 15ml spoons/2 tablespoons fresh oregano,
chopped
175g/6oz cream cheese, softened
100g/4oz fresh breadcrumbs
50g/2oz hazelnuts, chopped
50g/2oz butter, melted

Rinse and pat dry the turkey. Season the cavity. Mix the onion, garlic, lemon rind and juice, oregano, cheese, breadcrumbs and nuts. Place the turkey with the neck towards you. Insert your fingers between the flesh and breast skin. Carefully loosen the skin from the breast and thighs. Spread the stuffing evenly under the skin, reshape and truss the bird. Weigh the bird. Allow 20 minutes per 450g/1lb cooking time plus 20 minutes. Place in a roasting tin with a rack and brush all over with the melted butter. Roast at 190°C/375°F/Gas 5 until golden and tender. Allow to cool completely. Wrap in kitchen foil and carve at the picnic site for a really glamorous centrepiece.

CHICKEN GALANTINE

MAIN DISH   SERVES UP TO 12

1 chicken or capon (approximately 2kg/4½lb)
175g/6oz sliced tongue
750g/1½lb sausagemeat
100g/4oz streaky bacon, rinds removed and chopped
100g/4oz fresh white breadcrumbs
1 lemon, grated rind and juice
2 × 5ml spoons/2 teaspoons dried mixed herbs
1 egg
100g/4oz sliced cooked ham
75g/3oz stuffed green olives, chopped
50g/2oz butter, melted
1 × 15ml spoon/1 tablespoon oil

Bone the bird without breaking the skin. Trim the legs to the lowest joint. Set the bird on a board, breast side down. Make a cut from the parsons nose, along the backbone to the neck vent. This is the only time you will cut the skin. Using a sharp knife carefully cut the flesh away from the bones of the carcase working either side of the first cut until you reach the leg joints. Cut through these and continue cutting the flesh away from the carcass, cutting through the wing joints until you are able to lift away the main carcass of the bird. Scrape down around the top leg and wing bones to the joints, cut through and remove the bones.

Spread the bird out flat on the board and cover with polythene film. Beat several times with a rolling pin to even out the flesh. Season the flesh and cover it with a layer of sliced tongue.

In a large bowl place the sausagemeat, bacon, breadcrumbs, rind and juice, herbs and egg. Knead together with the hands until evenly blended. Form into a flattened log shape and place down the centre of the bird from neck to tail. Cover the stuffing with slices of ham and finally lay a line of chopped olives down the centre of the ham. Season well. Bring the sides of the bird up over the stuffing to enclose it and sew up the skin using a large needle and coarse thread. Turn the bird over and reshape it with the hands. Truss the bird round the legs and wings. Season and set it on a large piece of kitchen foil. Brush all over with the butter and oil.

Enclose it in the foil and weigh the parcel to calculate cooking time.

Place the parcel in a roasting tin and cook at 180°C/350°F/Gas 4 for 30 minutes per 450g/1lb. Open the foil and baste well and continue to cook for a further 40 minutes until the skin is golden. To test if the bird is cooked, insert a skewer; juices should run clear when cooked. Remove from the foil and leave on a roasting rack to drain and cool. Remove the thread from the skin. Chill.

For a picnic with several people, pack the galantine in a rigid container and carve into slices on site. Alternatively, for two (or three) people, carve slices at home and wrap individually or arrange on a platter and cover with cling film.

CELERY, HAM AND CARROT SALAD

SERVES 4-6

8 sticks celery, trimmed and sliced
6 carrots, coarsely grated
8 slices cooked ham, cut into strips
3 × 15ml spoons/3 tablespoons capers, drained
DRESSING
300ml/½ pint single cream
1 lemon, finely grated rind and 1 × 15ml spoon/
1 tablespoon of juice
6 × 15ml spoons/6 tablespoons natural yoghurt
pinch ground cumin
freshly-ground black pepper

Place the celery, carrots, ham and capers in a container. Blend the dressing ingredients together and season with freshly-ground black pepper. Mix into the salad and chill well before packing.

COLD PARSLIED RATATOUILLE SALAD

SERVES 6-8

1 aubergine, thickly sliced
salt
3 × 15ml spoons/3 tablespoons olive oil
2 onions, peeled, sliced
450g/1 lb courgettes, sliced
1 red pepper, cored, deseeded and sliced
1 green pepper, cored, deseeded and sliced
400g/14oz tin tomatoes
2 × 5ml spoons/2 teaspoons dried oregano
GARNISH
croûtons
3 × 15ml spoons/3 tablespoons fresh parsley,
chopped
1 × 15ml spoon/1 tablespoon fresh basil, chopped
black olives
freshly-ground black pepper

Layer the aubergine slices in a colander with salt. Allow to stand and drain for 30 minutes.

Heat the oil in a large pan. Fry the onion for 3 minutes. Stir in the courgette and pepper slices and continue to fry for 5 minutes. Rinse the aubergine and add to the pan with the tomatoes and herbs. Season generously with freshly-ground black pepper. Cover the pan and cook gently for 45 minutes. Remove from the heat, cover and cool. Pack into a large container. Chill thoroughly. Serve scattered with croûtons, parsley, basil and olives, which have been separately packed.

CRUNCHY CAULIFLOWER SALAD

SERVES 2-4

1 large head broccoli
1 small cauliflower
1 red pepper, cored, deseeded and cut into strips
75g/3oz smoked ham, cut into shreds
50g/2oz pinenuts, toasted
DRESSING
2 × 15ml spoons/2 tablespoons raspberry vinegar
4 × 15ml spoons/4 tablespoons olive oil
pinch of salt
pinch of sugar
1 × 5ml spoon/1 teaspoon wholegrain mustard
1 × 15ml spoon/1 tablespoon fresh parsley, chopped

Cut the broccoli and cauliflower into tiny florets. Steam them with the red pepper for 2 to 3 minutes until very lightly cooked and tender but still crunchy. Cool. Mix with the ham and pinenuts. Mix the dressing ingredients together and pour over the salad. Chill before serving.

TORTELLINI AND SOUR CREAM SALAD

SERVES 4-6

225g/8oz fresh spinach and ham-stuffed tortellini
85ml/3fl oz sour cream
85ml/3fl oz thick Greek yoghurt
2 × 15ml spoons/2 tablespoons mayonnaise
2 × 15ml spoons/2 tablespoons fresh mint, chopped
½ × 5ml spoon/½ teaspoon coriander, freshly ground
ground black pepper, salt

Cook the fresh tortellini in boiling salted water for 4 to 6 minutes until tender. Drain and refresh in cold water. Drain.

Blend the sour cream, yoghurt, mayonnaise, mint and coriander. Season with ground black pepper and salt. Stir in the pasta and chill. Pack the salad in a rigid container.

WATERCRESS AND PALM HEART SALAD

SERVES 4-6

8 small tinned palm hearts, drained and sliced
1 bunch watercress, trimmed
4 thin slices smoked ham, cut into strips
4 tomatoes, skinned, sliced
DRESSING
2 × 15ml spoons/2 tablespoons olive oil
1 × 15ml spoon/1 tablespoon red wine vinegar
1 × 15ml spoon/1 teaspoon wholegrain mustard
few drops lemon juice
pinch sugar

Gently combine the salad ingredients and pack in a rigid container. Chill. Place the dressing ingredients in a small screw-topped jar and pack separately. Shake the jar to blend the dressing and pour over the salad just before serving.

BLUE CHEESE, BACON AND APPLE SALAD

SERVES 4

225g/8oz blue brie, rind removed and diced
225g/8oz streaky bacon, rinds removed
2 red-skinned apples, cored and chopped
1 × 15ml spoon/1 tablespoon lemon juice
50g/2oz hazelnuts, halved
85ml/3fl oz sour cream

Place the cheese in a container. Grill the bacon and cut into small pieces. Mix with the cheese and add the apples, tossed in the lemon juice, the nuts and cream. Season with black pepper. Chill. Keep cool as possible when transporting.

CŒUR À LA CRÈME

MAKES 8-12

225g/8oz cottage cheese
225g/8oz cream cheese
450ml/¾ pint double cream, whipped
4 × 15ml spoons/4 tablespoons caster sugar
4 egg whites
TO SERVE
single cream
fresh fruit
caster sugar

Traditionally, heart-shaped china moulds with draining holes are used for this dessert. Press the cheeses through a fine nylon sieve. Gently fold in the cream and sugar. Whisk the egg whites stiffly and fold in. Line the moulds with pieces of scalded muslin. Divide the mixture between the moulds and stand them on plates to drain overnight in the refrigerator.

Transport the creams in the moulds. Unmould just before serving and peel away the muslin. Serve with single cream, sugar and fresh fruit of the season – strawberries or raspberries are ideal.

SPECIAL SUMMER PUDDING

SERVES 6-8

1 madeira cake, 20cm/8 inch square
225g/8oz raspberries
225g/8oz redcurrants, stalks removed
225g/8oz strawberries, hulled
1 lemon, grated rind only
150ml/¼ pint red wine
2 × 15ml spoons/2 tablespoons port
75g/3oz caster sugar

Cut the cake into 4 thin layers. Cut each layer into long triangles and use these to line a 1.7l/3 pint pudding basin or mould. Press any trimmings into the holes to make a complete lining of sponge cake. Reserve enough cake to cover the top of the basin.

Place the raspberries and redcurrants in a large bowl. Cut the strawberries in half and add them to the bowl with the lemon rind.

Pour the wine, port and sugar into another pan and heat gently until the sugar dissolves. Add the fruit and simmer for 5 minutes. Remove from the heat and cool slightly. Taste for sweetness and add a little more sugar if liked. Spoon the fruit and its juices into the prepared basin or mould and cover with the reserved cake. Place a saucer on top and weight it. Chill overnight.

Transport the pudding in the basin. Turn out just before serving. Serve with whipped cream.

AUTUMN BOUNTY

The balmy days of autumn are often warm enough to spend outside picnicking. With fruit and nuts growing ripe on the trees and blackberries taking over the hedgerows, it is also the time to go out gathering – so why not combine the two.

Serious fruit-pickers will have developed an appetite by lunchtime, so provide a selection of tempting dishes. Smoked Trout Baklava cut into diamond shapes, Ham and Cheese Croissants, Ricotta and Smoked Salmon Parcels and vegetable Crudités with Garlic and Walnut Dip would make a mouth-watering display.

Follow with fruit-laden desserts, perhaps an Open Cherry Pie and a Baked Plum Cheesecake. Then, for sustenance through the afternoon, hold back some Crunchy Caramel Cones, and Coffee Brazil Snaps for good measure.

POTTED TONGUE

SERVES 6

225g/8oz unsalted butter, melted
225g/8oz sliced tongue, chopped
pinch ground allspice
pinch ground nutmeg
1 × 15ml spoon/1 tablespoon brandy

Allow the melted butter to stand so that the clear golden butter floats on the sediment of whey and salt. Spoon off the butter and discard the cloudy sediment. Pound or mince the tongue with two-thirds of the butter. Add the spices, brandy and plenty of freshly-ground black pepper. Press this mixture firmly into small pots and smooth the surface level. Pour the remaining clarified butter over the tongue and chill until set and sealed. Cover with foil to transport.

Serve with crackers and watercress.

SMOKED TROUT BAKLAVA

MAKES ABOUT 30

1 bunch spring onions, sliced
25g/1oz butter
1 bunch watercress, trimmed and chopped
1-2 × 15ml spoons/1-2 tablespoons creamed horseradish
4 smoked trout fillets, skinned and flaked
750g/1½lb curd cheese
12 sheets filo pastry
50g/2oz butter, melted

Fry the spring onions in the butter for 3 minutes. Remove from the heat and stir in the watercress. Set aside. Mix the horseradish with the fish. Soften the curd cheese and blend in the onions and watercress. Stir in the fish mixture.

Butter an 18 × 28cm/7 × 11 inch baking tin and cut six sheets of pastry to fit inside the tin. Butter each sheet in turn and place in the bottom of the tin. Spread the filling over and cover with six more sheets of buttered pastry. Cut the top layer of pastry into small diamond shapes (about 30) and brush again with butter. Bake at 200°C/400°F/Gas 6 for 35 to 40 minutes until golden. Cool in the tin for 20 minutes.

Cut the baklava into diamond shapes and cool on a wire rack. Pack, interleaved with greaseproof paper, in a rigid container.

HAM AND CHEESE CROISSANTS

MAKES 12

25g/1 oz fresh yeast
250ml/8 fl oz lukewarm milk
50g/2 oz melted butter, cooled
1 egg, beaten
1 × 5ml spoon/1 teaspoon salt
450g/1 lb strong plain flour
175g/6 oz butter blended with 25g/1 oz plain flour
FILLING
2 slices ham, chopped
75g/3 oz Gruyère cheese, grated
beaten egg, to glaze

Cream the yeast with the milk, add the melted butter, egg and salt. Pour into a well in the flour and mix to a smooth dough. Knead until smooth and elastic (about 10 minutes). Place in an oiled polythene bag and leave to rise in a warm place until doubled in size – about 1 hour.

Knead the dough lightly to remove the air and roll it out to a 20 × 46cm/8 × 18 inch rectangle. Have a short end nearest you. Dot a third of the blended butter and flour mixture over the top two-thirds of the dough rectangle. Fold the bottom third of the dough up over the middle third and the top third down over that. Press the edges together with the rolling pin to seal. Turn the dough through 90° to the left. Return to the polythene bag and chill for 15 minutes. Repeat the process twice more using the remaining blended butter, then repeat the rolling and folding twice more without butter. Be sure to chill the dough between each process so that the fat does not melt. Finally, cut the dough in half. Roll each piece evenly to a 60 × 20cm/24 × 8 inch strip. Cut each strip into long triangles.

Mix the ham and cheese and divide into 12 portions. Place a portion at the wide end of each dough triangle. Roll up the triangles from the filled end to the tip. Curve into crescent shapes. Place on greased baking sheets. Cover with oiled polythene and prove in a warm place for 30 minutes. Brush with beaten egg and bake at 220°C/425°F/Gas 7 for 10 to 15 minutes.

Wrap in absorbent kitchen paper while still hot and transport in an insulated box to the picnic.

CREAMY HAM CROUSTADES

MAKES 12

1 large white loaf, crusts removed
100g/4 oz butter, melted
FILLING
75g/3 oz cream cheese
120ml/4 fl oz single cream
100g/4 oz cooked ham, chopped
freshly-ground black pepper
2 × 15ml spoons/2 tablespoons fresh chives, chopped
2 × 15ml spoons/2 tablespoons pistachio nuts, chopped
2 × 5ml spoons/2 teaspoons mild wholegrain mustard
GARNISH
paprika pepper
mustard and cress

Cut the loaf into slices 5cm/2 inch thick. Cut each slice into two 5cm/2 inch squares. Set the bread cubes on a baking sheet. Cut holes in the cubes, 6mm/¼ inch from the edges and nearly through to the base, to make box shapes, scooping out the crumb. Brush the boxes inside and out with the melted butter. Bake at 200°C/400°F/Gas 6 for 15 to 20 minutes until golden and crisp. Allow to cool on a wire rack. To make the filling, blend the cream cheese and single cream. Add salt and freshly-ground black pepper. Stir in the ham, chives, nuts and mustard. Chill.

Just before packing, spoon the filling into the croustades and garnish each with a sprinkling of paprika and a few leaves of mustard and cress. Pack into a rigid container and keep as cool as possible.

VARIATION *Cheese and Mustard Cups*
Make as for the Creamy Ham Croustades but fill with a cheese and mustard mixture.

To make the filling, melt 25g/1 oz butter in a small pan and stir in 1 × 15ml spoon/1 tablespoon plain flour and cook for 1 minute. Blend in 1 × 15ml spoon/1 tablespoon wholegrain mustard and 150ml/¼ pint milk and cook to a smooth sauce. Stir in 50g/2 oz each of cream cheese and grated Wensleydale cheese and season with freshly-ground white pepper. Allow to cool.

VEGETABLE CRUDITÉS WITH GARLIC AND WALNUT DIP

SERVES 6

1 small cauliflower, broken into florets
1 green pepper, cored, deseeded and cut into strips
2 red-skinned apples, cored, sliced and tossed in lemon juice
3 sticks celery, trimmed, cut into sticks
3 carrots, cut into thin sticks
¼ cucumber, cut into thin sticks
DIP
175ml/6fl oz mayonnaise
150ml/¼ pint double cream, whipped
1 clove garlic, crushed in a little salt
25g/1 oz walnuts, finely ground
1 × 5ml spoon/1 teaspoon lemon juice
freshly-ground white pepper

Prepare the vegetables and fruit and sprinkle them with a few drops of water. Seal them in polythene bags and chill. Transport the vegetables in the bag.

To make the dip, fold the mayonnaise into the cream. Stir in the garlic, walnuts and lemon juice. Add plenty of freshly-ground white pepper. Chill in a sealed container and serve with the vegetables.

VARIATION   *Green Herb Dip*
Replace the garlic and walnuts with 2 × 15ml spoons/2 tablespoons chopped watercress, 1 × 15ml spoon/1 tablespoon fresh chopped parsley and 1 × 15ml spoon/1 tablespoon fresh chopped chervil. Make the dip in the way described.

VEAL AND TONGUE TERRINE

SERVES 6-8

PASTRY
350g/12 oz plain flour
1 × 5ml spoon/1 teaspoon allspice
175g/6 oz butter
1 egg, beaten
water to mix
FILLING
450g/1 lb lean veal, cut in thick slices
450g/1 lb cooked tongue, cut in thick slices
3 × 15ml spoons/3 tablespoons fresh parsley, chopped
1 × 15ml spoon/1 tablespoon mint jelly
1 lemon, grated rind and juice
120ml/4fl oz white wine
beaten egg, to glaze
TO FINISH
1 × 5ml spoon/1 teaspoon gelatine

Sift the flour and allspice into a large bowl and rub in the butter. Add the egg and just enough cold water to bind to a dough. Knead lightly until smooth and use three-quarters of the dough to line a 900g/2lb loaf tin. Combine all the ingredients for the filling in a large bowl. Cover and marinate for 2 hours. Drain the meat, reserving the marinade and layer the meat into the prepared loaf tin. Use the remaining pastry to make a lid and use any trimmings for decorations. Crimp and seal the crust and make a hole in the lid to allow the steam to escape. Brush with beaten egg. Bake at 220°C/425°F/Gas 7 for 20 minutes. Reduce the heat to 180°C/350°F/Gas 4 for 1½ hours.

Dissolve the gelatine in the reserved juice of the marinade and pour into the terrine as it cools. Pack the terrine in foil and serve in slices at the picnic or, alternatively, cut slices before leaving home and wrap individually.

RICOTTA AND SMOKED SALMON PARCELS

MAKES 16

225g/8 oz ricotta cheese
75g/3 oz smoked salmon trimmings, chopped
2 × 15ml spoons/2 tablespoons fresh parsley,
chopped
½ lemon, grated rind only
1-2 × 5ml spoon/1-2 teaspoons pink peppercorns,
drained
freshly-ground black pepper
8 sheets filo pastry
75g/3 oz butter, melted

Blend the cheese with the salmon, parsley, lemon rind and peppercorns. Season to taste with black pepper. Divide this filling into 16 portions.

Work with one sheet of pastry at a time and keep the rest under a damp cloth. Divide a sheet of pastry in half lengthways. Brush each half with butter and lay a portion of the filling at a short end of each. For each piece of pastry follow the same procedure: fold both long sides in towards the centre, over the filling at one end. Roll the filled end along the strip to make a neat parcel. Brush with more butter and place on a baking sheet. Repeat with the remaining pastry and filling.

Bake the parcels at 200°C/400°F/Gas 6 for 10 to 12 minutes until golden-brown and crispy. Cool on a wire rack. Pack the parcels in a rigid container for transportation.

FRANGIPANE TART

SERVES 6-8

1 quantity sweet shortcrust pastry (see Open Cherry
Pies, page 84)
FILLING
5 × 15ml spoons/5 tablespoons good-quality
raspberry jam
100g/4oz butter
100g/4oz caster sugar
2 eggs, beaten
100g/4oz ground almonds
15g/½oz plain flour
few drops almond essence
50g/2oz ready-made marzipan, coarsely grated

Roll out the pastry and use it to line a 23cm/9 inch
flan tin or dish. Spread the base of the pastry flan
with jam.

To make the filling, cream the butter and sugar
together until light and fluffy. Gradually beat in
the eggs a little at a time. Fold in the ground
almonds, flour and essence. Spread the mixture in
the pastry case and set the flan on a baking sheet.
Bake at 190°C/375°F/Gas 5 for 40 to 45 minutes
until risen and spongy. Scatter the marzipan flakes
over the flan and return to the oven for 5 minutes.
Cool.

Transport the tart in the tin. Serve sliced with
fresh fruit cut into pieces.

HONEY AND SULTANA DROP SCONES

MAKES 18-20

225g/8oz self-raising flour
½ × 5ml spoon/½ teaspoon baking powder
2 eggs, beaten
25g/1oz butter, melted
2 × 15ml spoons/2 tablespoons thick honey
300ml/½ pint milk
25g/1oz sultanas
oil for cooking

Place the flour, baking powder, eggs, butter, honey
and milk in a liquidiser or food processor and
blend until very smooth. Stir in the sultanas. Heat
a heavy-based frying pan or griddle and brush
lightly with oil. Drop spoonfuls of the mixture onto
the griddle and cook over a medium heat until
bubbles appear on the surface. Turn the scones
over and cook the other side for 2 to 3 minutes.
Cool on a clean tea towel. Butter the scones and
pack in a rigid container or box, interleaved with
greaseproof paper. Serve buttered.

PINENUT SAVOURY BREAD

MAKES 1 LARGE LOAF

25g/1 oz fresh yeast
450ml/¾ pint lukewarm milk
750g/1½ lb strong plain flour
2 × 5ml spoon/2 teaspoons salt
1 × 15ml spoon/1 tablespoon sugar
25g/1 oz butter
225g/8 oz smoked streaky bacon, rinds removed
25g/1 oz pinenuts
milk, to glaze

Blend the yeast in the milk. Sift the flour, salt and
sugar into a warmed bowl. Rub in the butter and
pour in the yeast mixture. Mix to a smooth dough
and knead for 10 minutes on a lightly floured
surface until soft and smooth. Place in an oiled
polythene bag in a warm place and leave to rise
until doubled in size.

Grill the bacon until crisp and chop.

Remove the dough from the bag and knead in
the bacon and pinenuts. Cut the dough into 5
pieces and form each into a small roll. Pack the
rolls side by side in a large greased loaf tin. Cover
with oiled polythene film and allow to prove until
the dough reaches the top of the tin. Remove the
film, brush with milk and bake at 230°C/450°F/Gas
8 for 45 to 50 minutes. Cover the loaf with foil if it
begins to brown too quickly. Allow to cool. Slice
and butter the bread and pack in a box or tin.

MARMALADE FRENCH APPLE FLAN

SERVES 4-6

PASTRY
175g/6 oz plain flour
75g/3 oz butter
25g/1 oz icing sugar
1 egg yolk
FILLING
3 cooking apples, peeled, cored and roughly chopped
3 × 15ml spoons/3 tablespoons rough cut marmalade
1 orange, finely grated rind and juice
TOPPING
1 dessert apple, quartered, cored and thinly sliced
3 × 15ml spoons/3 tablespoons marmalade
1 × 15ml spoon/1 tablespoon lemon juice

To make the pastry, sift the flour into a large bowl
and rub in the butter until it resembles fine
breadcrumbs. Stir in the sugar and just enough
egg yolk to make a firm dough. Chill for 30
minutes. Line a 23cm/9 inch flan tin or dish with
the pastry. Chill again for 30 minutes then bake
blind for 15 to 20 minutes until the crust is
golden-brown. Cool in the tin or dish. To make the
filling, place all the ingredients plus 1 × 15ml
spoon/1 tablespoon of water into a tightly lidded
pan and heat gently until the apple is cooked to a
pulp. Beat until smooth, then cool. Spread into
the base of the pastry case.

To make the topping, arrange the apple slices
over the surface of the filling. Place the marmalade
and lemon juice in a small pan and bring to the
boil. Press through a sieve and brush over the
apple and crust of the flan. Transport in the tin.
Serve with cream, or thick yoghurt if liked.

COFFEE BRAZIL SNAPS

MAKES 20

50g/2oz butter
100g/4oz plain flour
75g/3oz caster sugar
50g/2oz brazil nuts, finely ground
½ egg, beaten
ICING
75g/3oz icing sugar
1 × 5ml spoon/1 teaspoon coffee essence
crushed coffee sugar crystals

Rub the butter into the flour. Stir in the sugar, nuts and egg and knead to a smooth dough. Form into a 5cm/2inch square-shaped parcel and wrap in foil. Chill for 1 hour until firm.

With a sharp knife, cut thin slices of dough. Place them on greased baking sheets and chill for 30 minutes more. Bake at 200°C/400°F/Gas 6 for 6 to 8 minutes. Allow to cool on the baking sheets for a few minutes then remove to a wire rack.

To make the icing, blend together the icing sugar, essence and just enough water to make a thick smooth mixture. Brush over the biscuits and sprinkle with crushed sugar crystals. Allow to set.

Pack in a rigid container, interleaved with greaseproof paper.

OPEN CHERRY PIES

MAKES 14

SWEET SHORTCRUST PASTRY
225g/8oz plain flour
100g/4oz butter
1 × 15ml spoon/1 tablespoon caster sugar
1 egg, beaten
FILLING
1 × 15ml spoon/1 tablespoon ground almonds
450g/1lb fresh or bottled cherries, stoned
4-6 × 15ml spoons/4-6 tablespoons redcurrant jelly, warmed
DECORATION
mint sprigs

Sift the flour into a bowl. Rub in the butter finely. Stir the sugar into the egg until dissolved. Add just enough of the egg mixture to the flour to make a soft dough. Chill for 15 minutes then knead lightly. Roll out on a lightly floured surface and cut out 7.5cm/3inch rounds with a pastry cutter. Use the rounds to line bun tins and prick each well with a fork. Chill for 30 minutes.

Bake at 190°C/375°F/Gas 5 for 10 to 15 minutes until just golden. Cool in the tins for 15 minutes then remove to a wire rack.

Sprinkle a little of the ground almonds in each pastry case. Fill with the stoned cherries. Spoon or brush the jelly over the fruit to seal it. Decorate each pie with a sprig of mint.

Pack the pies in a rigid container interleaved with greaseproof paper. Keep as cold as possible until ready to serve.

VARIATION *Raspberry Tartlets*
Make as for the Open Cherry Pies but use fresh raspberries and top with raspberry jelly.

ALMOND-FILLED MERINGUES

MAKES 18

1 egg white
50g/2oz icing sugar, sifted
FILLING
25g/1oz sugar
2 × 15ml spoons/2 tablespoons water
1 egg yolk
50g/2oz unsalted butter
few drops almond essence, or 1 teaspoon Amaretto
liqueur
DECORATION
75g/3oz blanched almonds, finely chopped

Whisk the egg white stiffly in a bowl. Set the bowl over a pan of simmering water. Add the sugar and whisk continuously until the mixture is shiny and very stiff. Remove the bowl from the heat and whisk until cool. Pipe, or spoon, the meringue into small round heaps on greased and lined baking sheets. Bake at 150°C/300°F/Gas 2 for 1½ hours until crisp. Cool on wire racks.

To make the filling, dissolve the sugar in the water in a small pan over gentle heat. Bring to the boil, without stirring and boil until the temperature reaches 110°C/225°F. Gradually whisk the bubbling syrup into the egg yolk in a thin stream. Continue to whisk until cool and thick. Gradually whisk in pieces of softened butter until the mixture is thick and glossy. Finally whisk in the almond essence or Amaretto liqueur.

Sandwich the meringue spheres together in pairs with the filling miture. Spread the remaining filling round the outside of the meringue balls and roll them in the chopped almonds. Place each sphere in a small paper case and pack in one layer in a rigid container.

PARIS BREST GÂTEAUX

SERVES 6

150ml/¼ pint water
50g/2oz butter
65g/2½oz strong plain flour, sifted
2 eggs, beaten
egg white, to glaze
15g/½oz flaked almonds
FILLING
25g/1oz whole blanched almonds
150g/5oz caster sugar
300ml/½ pint milk
few drops vanilla essence
2 egg yolks
1 × 15ml spoon/1 tablespoon flour
85ml/3fl oz double cream, whipped
DECORATION
icing sugar

Place the water and butter in a small pan and heat gently until the butter melts. Bring to the boil and quickly add the flour all at once. Beat over the heat until the flour comes away from the sides of the pan and a smooth paste forms. Cook for 1 minute more. Cool slightly. Gradually beat in just enough of the egg to make a firm, smooth glossy paste. Using a large piping bag and a 1cm/½inch plain nozzle pipe the paste into 6 small rings on a greased baking tray.

Bake at 220°C/425°F/Gas 7 for 30 minutes then cool for 10 minutes. Brush with egg white and sprinkle with the nuts. Return to the oven for 5 minutes until crisp and browned. Cool on a wire rack.

To make the filling, place the blanched almonds and 75g/3oz of the caster sugar in a heavy-based pan. Heat gently until the sugar melts. Stir briefly and pour onto an oiled baking sheet. Cool. Crush coarsely. Scald the milk. Whisk the egg yolks and remaining sugar together until thick and light. Stir in the flour. Whisk in the milk and pour into a pan. Bring to the boil, whisking all the time and cook for 2 minutes. Cover the surface with polythene film and allow to cool. Press the custard through a fine sieve, fold in the whipped cream and the crushed sugar and nut mixture.

Split the choux rings just before packing and fill with the mixture. Dust with a little icing sugar. Pack in a rigid container and keep cool.

CHOCOLATE CHIP MOUSSE

4 eggs, separated
100g/4oz caster sugar
100g/4oz bitter chocolate, melted
3 × 15ml spoons/3 tablespoons crème de cacao or brandy
15g/½oz gelatine, dissolved in 3 × 15ml spoons/3 tablespoons boiling water, cooled
300ml/½ pint double cream
50g/2oz white chocolate, chopped
DECORATION
single cream, chocolate curls

Whisk the egg yolks with the caster sugar until very thick and pale. Cool the melted chocolate and stir into the mixture with the liqueur or brandy. Stir in the gelatine. Whip the cream and fold in with the chopped chocolate. Pour the mousse into 6 or 8 individual pots and leave in a cool place to set. Transport in the pots. Serve with single cream and chocolate curls.

CRUNCHY CARAMEL CONES

MAKES 10-12

50g/2oz caster sugar
50g/2oz butter
50g/2oz golden syrup
50g/2oz plain flour, sifted
1 × 5ml spoon/1 teaspoon coriander seeds, roughly crushed
1 × 15ml spoon/1 tablespoon sesame seeds
1 × 5ml spoon/1 teaspoon lemon juice
100g/4oz plain chocolate, melted

Place the sugar, butter and syrup in a small saucepan and melt over a gentle heat. Bring to the boil and remove from the heat. Stir in the flour, seeds and lemon juice. Drop small spoonfuls of the mixture, well spaced, on baking sheets lined with non-stick baking paper. Bake, one sheet at a time, at 180°C/350°F/Gas 4 for 8 to 10 minutes until golden-brown round the edges.

Remove them from the paper with a palette knife and wrap each round an oiled cream horn tin to form a cone shape. When set (1 to 2 minutes), remove and cool on a wire rack. Dip the point of each cone into the chocolate and leave to cool until set.

Serve plain, or fill with sweetened whipped cream.

Pack the cones in a rigid container in one layer and keep cool and dry.

SULTANA STREUSEL CAKES

MAKES 16 PIECES

175g/6oz butter, softened
175g/6oz soft brown sugar.
3 eggs, beaten
175g/6oz self-raising flour
½ × 5ml spoon/½ teaspoon ground mixed spice
75g/3oz sultanas
TOPPING
100g/4oz butter
150g/5oz plain flour
50g/2oz ground hazelnuts
75g/3oz soft light brown sugar

Put the butter, sugar, eggs, flour, mixed spice and sultanas in a large bowl and beat well together for 3 minutes until smooth. Spread into a greased and lined 20cm/8 inch-square tin.

To make the topping, rub the butter into the flour until the mixture resembles breadcrumbs. Stir in the ground nuts and sugar. Sprinkle this crumble mixture over the cake mixture in the tin. Bake at 180°C/350°F/Gas 4 for 45 to 50 minutes. Leave in the tin for 15 minutes. Cut into bars and cool on a wire rack.

Pack in a rigid container.

BAKED PLUM CHEESECAKE

SERVES 8

BASE
50g/2oz butter, softened
50g/2oz caster sugar
1 egg, beaten
50g/2oz self-raising flour
2 × 5ml spoons/2 teaspoons milk
FILLING
350g/12oz ripe plums, stoned and quartered
225g/8oz curd cheese
100g/4oz cream cheese, softened
100g/4oz cottage cheese, sieved
50g/2oz caster sugar
2 eggs, beaten
150ml/¼ pint sour cream
DECORATION
fresh sliced plums

To make the base, beat together all the ingredients until smooth. Spread in a greased and lined 20cm/8inch loose-based cake tin. Bake at 190°C/375°F/Gas 5 for 20 minutes. Leave in the tin to cool.

To make the filling, arrange the plums over the sponge cake base. Beat together the remaining filling ingredients until smooth. Carefully pour over the plums. Return to the oven at 180°C/350°F/Gas 4 for 30 minutes until just set. Cool. Transport the Cheesecake in the tin.

Just before serving, remove the tin and paper and serve in slices with fresh plums and a little single cream if liked.

ROSE PETAL JELLY

MAKES 1kg/2lb

1kg/2lb cooking apples, washed, roughly chopped
600ml/1 pint water (approximately)
450g/1 lb preserving, or granulated, sugar to
600ml/1 pint of juice
petals from 3 freshly-picked pink roses
few drops rose water
few drops red food colouring, if liked

Place the apples in a large pan and pour in just enough water to cover. Bring to a simmer and cook for about 1 hour until soft and pulpy. Mash against the sides of the pan with a wooden spoon. Strain the fruit juice through a scalded jelly bag into a bowl. Do not squeeze the fruit but allow it to drip for at least 1 hour, or overnight.

Measure the strained juice into a clean pan. Bring to a slow simmer and add 450g/1 lb sugar per 600ml/1 pint of juice. Stir until the sugar has dissolved. Add three-quarters of the rose petals, bring to the boil and boil briskly until setting point is reached. Check for setting point by placing a small spoonful of mixture on a chilled saucer. After one minute, if a finger pushed against the jelly causes the surface to wrinkle then setting point has been reached. Remove the pan from the heat. Skim off the scum and rose petals.

Add the rosewater, colouring and remaining rose petals. Pour into small, clean, warm jars. Top immediately with waxed discs and cover with polythene film. Allow to cool.

Transport rose petal jelly in the jars. It is very good with freshly-baked scones, perhaps with a spoonful of thickly-whipped cream.

CREAMED CHOCOLATE DRINK

SERVES 6

900ml/1½ pints milk
150ml/¼ pint double cream
175g/6oz plain chocolate, broken into pieces
TO SERVE
whipped cream
ground cinnamon

Put the milk, cream and chocolate into a pan and gently heat until evenly blended and just below simmering point. Pour into a flask.

Take with you a small container of whipped cream and float a little of this on each serving, dusted with cinnamon if liked.

WINTER PICNICS

A sharp, bright winter's morning tempts people out-of-doors and provides another excuse for a sensational picnic. A selection of tantalizing snacks, hot soups and unusual casseroles should stir even the most sluggish appetites.

Spicy dishes like Cocktail Chicken Tandoori and Peppered Roast Beef make delicious appetizers. Serve them with hot Tomato Chowder if it is cold. For a hearty main course, the Cassoulet Pot, which is packed with chicken, vegetables, haricot beans, smoked pork sausage and bacon, is ideal. If the weather is mild, a selection of salads might be appropriate. Unusual ones like Creamy Pesto Tagliatelle Salad and Pink Grapefruit and Avocado Salad could be served with the impressive-looking Nutty Bacon Plait.

For a winter dish with a difference, supply large quantities of Orange and almond mince pies served with lashings of Brandied Cream or Cointreau Butter.

CREAMY CHEESE RISOTTO

SERVES 4

25g/1 oz butter
1 × 15ml spoon/1 tablespoon olive oil
350g/12 oz risotto rice
1 onion, finely chopped
900ml/1½ pints chicken stock
75g/3 oz Gruyère cheese, grated
75g/3 oz Emmental cheese, grated
1 × 15ml spoon/1 tablespoon Parmesan cheese
GARNISH
4 rashers streaky bacon, grilled crisp, crumbled

Melt the butter and oil in a large pan. Add the rice and onion and fry for 2 to 3 minutes. Pour in the stock, bring to the boil, stir and allow to simmer for 15 to 20 minutes until most of the stock has been absorbed but the rice is still creamy. Stir in the cheeses, season and heat through. Keep hot in a food flask and serve hot, sprinkled with crumbled bacon and with a green salad.

CASSOULET POT

MAIN DISH   SERVES 6

225g/8 oz haricot beans, soaked overnight in cold water
2 carrots, peeled and chopped
2 onions, peeled and chopped
2 sticks celery, chopped
1 bouquet garni
freshly-ground black pepper
225g/8 oz streaky bacon, without rinds, chopped
1 clove garlic, peeled and crushed
1 chicken, approximately 1kg/2½ lb jointed into 8 pieces
3 × 15ml spoons/3 tablespoons tomato purée
600ml/1 pint chicken stock
350g/12 oz smoked pork sausage, sliced
4 × 15ml spoons/4 tablespoons parsley, freshly chopped

Drain the beans and place in a large pan covered with fresh cold water. Bring to the boil and boil for 10 minutes. Reduce the heat to a simmer and add the carrots, onion, celery and bouquet garni. Season with freshly-ground black pepper, cover and simmer for 1 hour.

In another pan, fry the bacon in its own fat for 3 minutes. Add the garlic and cook for 1 minute. Add the chicken pieces and cook until the pieces are browned on all sides. Add the tomato purée and stock. Season and simmer for 40 minutes until the chicken is tender.

Remove the chicken skin and discard it. Cut the meat from the bones. Drain the beans and vegetables and place in an ovenproof casserole. Add the chicken meat. Skim the chicken cooking liquor and add to the pan with the the bacon. Stir in the sausage and parsley. Bake at 180°C/350°F/Gas 4 for 1 hour 15 minutes.

Remove from the oven and wrap the casserole in towels and put into an insulating bag.

Serve hot at the picnic with jacket potatoes, fresh from the oven, wrapped in foil and packed in a similar way to the cassoulet, and with pieces of crusty bread.

TOMATO CHOWDER

SERVES 6

2 × 15ml spoons/2 tablespoons oil
1 clove garlic, peeled and crushed
1 onion, finely chopped
2 sticks celery, thinly sliced
4 rashers streaky bacon, rinds removed, chopped
350g/12oz potatoes, peeled and cubed
3 × 15ml spoons/3 tablespoons tomato purée
4 tomatoes, skinned and chopped
sprig oregano
2 × 15ml spoons/2 tablespoons fresh parsley,
chopped
pinch of caster sugar
1 × 5ml spoon/1 teaspoon Worcestershire sauce
900ml/1½ pints chicken or vegetable stock
salt, freshly-ground black pepper

Heat the oil in a large pan and fry the garlic, onion, celery and bacon for 4 minutes. Stir in the potatoes and cook for 1 minute. Blend the tomato purée with the chopped tomatoes and herbs. Stir into the pan with the remaining ingredients. Season to taste with salt and freshly-ground black pepper. Simmer gently for about 10 minutes until the potatoes are tender.

Pour into a large flask for transportation. Serve hot with wholemeal rolls and butter.

CHICKEN NOODLE SOUP

SERVES 4-6

25g/1oz butter
100g/4oz button mushrooms, sliced
1 onion, peeled and chopped
1.1 litres/2 pints home-made chicken stock
2 cooked chicken quarters, skinned and boned
freshly-ground white pepper
50g/2oz vermicelli pasta
3 × 15ml spoons/3 tablespoons fresh parsley,
chopped

Heat the butter in a large pan. Fry the mushrooms and onion for 4 minutes. Add the stock and the chicken, torn into small pieces. Bring to the boil. Skim any fat from the surface. Season with freshly-ground white pepper and add the pasta. Simmer for 10 minutes. Stir in the parsley and pour into flasks for transportation.

CALZONE

SERVES 4-6

15g/½oz fresh yeast
300ml/½ pint lukewarm water
pinch of salt
pinch of sugar
350g/12oz strong plain flour
1 × 15ml spoon/1 tablespoon olive oil
FILLING
350g/12oz ricotta cheese
175g/6oz mozzarella cheese, grated
175g/6oz salami, shredded
3 × 15ml spoons/3 tablespoons fresh Parmesan
cheese, grated
3 eggs, beaten
salt, pepper

Dissolve the yeast in the water and stir in the salt and sugar. Pour the mixture into the flour with the oil and mix to a dough. Knead until very smooth and elastic – about 10 minutes. Cover with oiled polythene film and leave to rise in a warm place until doubled in size.

To make the filling, mix the ingredients together, reserving 1 × 15ml spoon/1 tablespoon of beaten egg for glazing. Add plenty of seasoning.

Knock back the risen dough and divide into 6 pieces. Roll a piece of dough out thinly on a lightly floured surface to make a 20cm/8 inch circle.

Place one-sixth of the filling on the dough and wet the edges of the circle. Fold one side of the dough over to make a half-circle shape and seal the edges. Place on a baking sheet and brush with a little egg yolk. Repeat with the remaining dough and filling. Bake at 220°C/425°F/Gas 7 for 10 to 15 minutes. Allow to cool, or keep warm and serve hot at the picnic.

MUSTARDY HAM IN PASTRY

MAIN DISH   SERVES 10-12

2.7kg/6lb piece boneless, cooked gammon joint
3 × 15ml spoons/3 tablespoons wholegrain mustard
2 × 15ml spoons/2 tablespoons redcurrant jelly
3 × 15ml spoons/3 tablespoons fresh parsley,
chopped
PASTRY
100g/4oz butter
100g/4oz shortening
pinch of salt
pinch of ground allspice
450g/1lb plain flour
iced water to mix
1 egg, beaten with a pinch of salt

Trim any fat from the meat. In a small bowl blend the mustard, jelly and parsley. Spread this evenly over the meat surface and leave it to stand.

Make the pastry by rubbing the butter and shortening into the salt, spices and flour. When the mixture resembles fine breadcrumbs stir in just enough water to mix to a firm dough. Roll out the pastry thinly on a lightly floured surface. Have it just large enough to enclose the meat. Place the meat in the centre of the pastry and bring up the sides of the pastry to make a neat parcel. Seal the joins with beaten egg and place the parcel with joins underneath on a greased baking sheet. Use the pastry trimmings to make leaves and flowers to decorate the parcel. Brush with beaten egg and chill for 30 minutes.

Bake at 200°C/400°F/Gas 6 for about 40 minutes until crisp and golden-brown. Cool on a wire rack.

Wrap in foil and transport whole. Carve in slices at the picnic. Serve with pickles and salad. Alternatively, carve the ham at home and wrap portions individually.

COCKTAIL CHICKEN TANDOORI

MAIN DISH   SERVES 6-8

6 chicken breasts, skinned, boned and cut into
chunks
2 × 15ml spoons/2 tablespoons lime or lemon juice
1 × 5ml spoon/1 teaspoon salt
1 × 15ml spoon/1 tablespoon oil
2 × 5ml spoons/2 teaspoons ground cardamom
2 × 5ml spoons/2 teaspoons ground cumin
1 × 5ml spoon/1 teaspoon mild ground chilli
2cm/1 inch piece fresh root ginger, peeled and
shredded
2 garlic cloves, peeled and crushed
150ml/¼ pint natural yoghurt
25g/1 oz butter

Place the chicken in a large shallow bowl. Sprinkle
the juice and salt over the chicken and mix it in
well. Heat the oil in a frying pan and add the
spices, ginger, and garlic. Cook, stirring for 3
minutes. Remove the pan from the heat and stir in
the yoghurt. Pour the mixture over the chicken and
cover. Marinate in the refrigerator overnight. The
following day, arrange the chicken pieces with the
marinade, in a large roasting tin. Dot with the
butter and cook at 220°C/425°F/Gas 7 for about 30
minutes or until tender. Baste occasionally during
cooking.

Cool and pack in rigid containers. Serve on
wooden cocktail sticks.

NUTTY BACON PLAIT

MAIN DISH   SERVES 6-8

1 onion, peeled and chopped
225g/8 oz streaky bacon, without rinds, chopped
50g/2 oz hazelnuts, chopped
2 carrots, peeled and grated
100g/4 oz fresh breadcrumbs
2 × 15ml spoons/2 tablespoons fresh parsley,
chopped
freshly ground coriander
450g/1 lb shortcrust pastry
1 egg, beaten
poppy seeds

Place the onion, bacon, nuts, carrots, breadcrumbs, parsley, seasoning and plenty of coriander in a large bowl and knead together. Form into
a 20cm/8 inch long roll. Chill until firm. Roll out
the pastry on a lightly floured surface to a 20 ×
30cm/8 × 12 inch rectangle. Place the bacon roll
along the centre of the pastry. Cut the exposed
pastry into strips, leaving them attached at the
centre. Fold the strips, from alternate sides, over
the bacon roll, making a plait effect. Place the plait
on an oiled baking sheet. Brush all over with
beaten egg and sprinkle with poppy seeds. Bake at
220°C/425°F/Gas 7 for 15 minutes. Reduce the
temperature to 180°C/350°F/Gas 4 for a further 40
minutes. Cool on a wire rack.

Transport the plait whole in a rigid container
and serve cut in thick slices with salad. Alternatively, slice at home and put pieces on serving
plates, covered with cling film.

BEEF PASTRY PARCELS

MAIN DISH   MAKES 12

6 thin slices of topside beef
50g/2oz butter
1 small onion, finely chopped
1 clove garlic, peeled and crushed
1 egg, beaten
25g/1oz fresh breadcrumbs
4 × 15ml spoons/4 tablespoons fresh herbs – parsley,
thyme, sage, mint, chopped
1 lemon, finely grated rind
freshly-ground black pepper
1 × 15ml spoon/1 tablespoon oil
hot beef stock
1 bouquet garni
150ml/¼ pint red wine
750g/1½lb puff pastry
1 egg, beaten to glaze

Spread out the pieces of meat. Melt the butter in a pan and fry the onion and garlic for 4 minutes. Transfer to a small bowl and mix in the egg, breadcrumbs, herbs and lemon rind. Divide the mixture between the slices of beef and spread it over them. Season with freshly-ground black pepper. Roll up each slice. Cut each roll in half to make 12 small rolls. Secure each with string or wooden cocktail sticks.

Heat the oil in a flameproof casserole and fry the rolls until browned on all sides. Add just enough stock to cover and add the bouquet garni and red wine. Cover and cook at 180°C/350°F/Gas 4 for 1¼ hours. Allow to cool in the stock. Drain the rolls and remove the string or cocktail sticks.

Roll out the pastry thinly and cut out 12 rectangles. Enclose each beef roll in a piece of pastry, brushing the edges of the pastry with egg to seal. Cut the pastry trimmings into long thin strips and use these to decorate the parcels. Place the parcels, joins underneath, on baking sheets and brush all over with beaten egg. Bake at 220°C/425°F/Gas 7 for 15 to 20 minutes. Cool on a wire rack.

Pack in a rigid container and serve with wholegrain mustard or horseradish relish.

PEPPERED ROAST BEEF

MAIN DISH   SERVES 8

1.4kg/3lb topside of beef, rolled and tied
1 × 15ml spoon/1 tablespoon white peppercorns
1 × 15ml spoon/1 tablespoon black peppercorns
1 × 15ml spoon/1 tablespoon coriander seeds
1 clove garlic, peeled and crushed
3 × 15ml spoons/3 tablespoons olive oil

Wipe the beef with absorbent kitchen paper and stand it in a roasting tin. Crush the peppercorns and coriander seeds in a pestle and mortar or use a rolling pin on a chopping board. Mix with the garlic and spread all over the surface of the meat. Cover and leave to marinate for 2 to 3 hours. Pour the oil over the meat and roast at 230°C/450°F/Gas 8 for 15 minutes then reduce the heat to 190°C/375°F/Gas 5 for about 45 minutes for medium rare meat. Cool on a wire rack.

Carve thinly just before packing into an airtight shallow, rigid container.

SERVING SUGGESTION   Serve a hot soup – such as Tomato Chowder (page 93) first, then rolled-up pieces of beef and paper-thin buttered brown bread.

CREAMY PESTO TAGLIATELLE SALAD

SERVES 6-8

100g/4 oz tagliatelle (raw weight)
2 cloves garlic, peeled and chopped
50g/2 oz pinenuts
3 × 15ml spoons/3 tablespoons fresh basil leaves or
parsley, chopped
25g/1 oz Parmesan cheese, freshly grated
3 × 15ml spoons/3 tablespoons olive oil
freshly-ground black pepper
150ml/¼ pint soured cream
4 × 15ml spoons/4 tablespoons natural yoghurt

Cook the tagliatelle in plenty of salted boiling water until just tender. Drain, rinse in cold water, drain again and cool.

Place the garlic, pinenuts and herbs in a blender and blend finely. Stir in the cheese and gradually stir in the oil. Season with freshly-ground black pepper. Stir in the soured cream and yoghurt. Pour over the pasta and toss to coat evenly. Transport in a rigid container. Serve with hot rolls.

PINK GRAPEFRUIT AND AVOCADO SALAD

SERVES 6

2 pink grapefruit
1 orange
100g/4oz smoked cheese
1 large avocado pear
¼ small head Chinese leaves, shredded
25g/1oz walnuts, coarsely chopped

Peel the fruit and remove all the pith. Cut the fruit into segments, catching the juice in a small bowl. Cut the cheese into thin sticks. Peel and stone the avocado pear. Cut into slices and dip in the collected fruit juice to prevent discolouration. Mix together the citrus fruits and any remaining juice, the cheese, avocado, Chinese leaves and walnuts. Chill and transport in a sealed container. Keep the salad cold.

FRENCH BEANS VINAIGRETTE

SERVES 6-8

450g/1 lb French (or Kenyan) beans, trimmed
DRESSING
4 × 15ml spoons/4 tablespoons olive oil
2 × 15ml spoons/2 tablespoons white wine vinegar
pinch of caster sugar
pinch of mustard powder
1 × 15ml spoon/1 tablespoon fresh parsley, chopped
1 hard-boiled egg, shelled

Cook the beans in boiling water until tender but still crisp. Drain.

Whisk together the dressing ingredients, except the egg, and pour over the beans while they are still hot. Allow to cool in the dressing, turning them occasionally to coat them. Pack into a shallow container.

Separate the egg yolk from the white. Finely chop the egg white and press the yolk through a sieve. Sprinkle the egg over the beans. Seal and chill before transporting.

ORANGE AND ALMOND MINCE PIES

MAKES 18

PASTRY
225g/8oz plain flour
50g/2oz ground almonds
25g/1oz icing sugar, sifted
1 orange, finely grated rind
175g/6oz butter
1 egg yolk
25g/1oz blanched almonds, chopped
½ jar mincemeat
1 egg white
caster sugar

To make the pastry, mix the flour, almonds, sugar and orange peel in a large bowl. Rub in the butter and stir in the egg yolk to make a firm dough. Add a very little water if necessary. Knead lightly until smooth. Wrap in polythene film and chill for 20 minutes.

Mix the chopped almonds with the mincemeat. Roll the dough out thinly, cut out about 18 rounds and use these to line bun tins. Place a spoonful of mincemeat in each pastry shell.

From the re-rolled pastry trimmings, stamp out small stars using a petit fours cutter. Place a star on the centre of the mincemeat in each pie. Brush each with a little egg white and sprinkle with caster sugar. Bake at 190°C/375°F/Gas 5 for 12 to 15 minutes until golden-brown. Cool on a wire rack or, for hot pies, pack them into a tin immediately, interleaved with absorbent kitchen paper. Wrap the tin in tea-towels, then put the tin in an insulating bag.

Mince pies are good served with Cointreau Butter or Brandied Cream.

Cointreau Butter Cream 75g/3oz butter with 50g/2oz icing sugar and 25g/1oz caster sugar. Gradually whisk in 3 × 15ml spoons/3 tablespoons of Cointreau, drop by drop until it is absorbed.

Brandied Cream Whisk together 150ml/¼ pint double cream and 150ml/¼ pint single cream and 1 × 15ml spoon/1 tablespoon caster sugar, with a few drops vanilla essence and 1 × 15ml spoon/1 tablespoon brandy. Pack into sealed containers.

TIPSY WINTER FRUIT SALAD

SERVES 4-6

2 (225g/8oz) packets dried mixed fruit salad (or choose a mixture of dried apricots, pears, peaches and apples)
1 lemon, grated rind and juice
1 orange, grated rind and juice
1.2 litres/2 pints strong black tea
1 cinnamon stick
3 × 15ml spoons/3 tablespoons rum or sherry
sugar, to taste

Place the dried fruit in a large bowl. Add the fruit rinds and juices and pour over the tea. Leave to soak overnight. Next day, add the cinnamon stick and simmer gently for 20 to 30 minutes until the fruit is soft and tender. Stir in the rum or sherry, remove the cinnamon and add sugar to taste. Serve chilled with natural yoghurt.

RUM BABAS

MAKES 8

1 × 15ml spoon/1 tablespoon caster sugar
3 × 15ml spoons/3 tablespoons lukewarm milk
2 × 5ml spoons/2 teaspoons dried yeast
100g/4oz strong plain flour
pinch of salt
2 eggs, beaten
50g/2oz butter, melted
50g/2oz currants
RUM SYRUP
200ml/⅓ pint water
75g/3oz sugar
1 × 5ml spoon/1 teaspoon lemon juice
3 × 15ml spoons/3 tablespoons rum
DECORATION
4 × 15ml spoons/4 tablespoons apricot jam, warmed
and sieved
whipped cream, to serve

Dissolve a pinch of the sugar in the milk in a jug and sprinkle the dried yeast over it. Whisk with a fork for a few seconds. Leave in a warm place for 15 minutes until the mixture is very frothy. Sift the flour and salt into a large warmed bowl. Pour the yeast liquid into the flour. Beat the remaining sugar with the eggs and pour into the flour with the melted butter. Mix to gradually incorporate the flour. Beat for 2 minutes until a smooth batter is formed. Cover and leave to rest for 10 minutes. Beat the dough thoroughly for 5 minutes. Beat in the currants. Lightly grease 8 baba tins or dariole moulds. Pour the dough into the tins and set them on a baking sheet. Cover with oiled polythene film. Leave to rise in a warm place for 30 to 40 minutes until the dough reaches the top of the tins.

Bake at 230°C/450°F/Gas 8 for 4 to 5 minutes then lower the temperature to 180°C/350°F/Gas 4 for 5 minutes more. Turn out the babas, clean the tins with absorbent kitchen paper and return the babas to their tins ready for soaking with syrup.

To make the syrup, place the water, sugar and lemon juice in a small pan and heat gently until dissolved. Bring to the boil and boil for 10 minutes. Cool for 5 minutes. Stir in the rum. Prick the babas all over with a skewer. Pour the syrup over them. Let the syrup soak in and leave until completely cooled. Turn out and brush with jam.

Pack in a rigid container and serve with sweetened whipped cream and a little fresh fruit.

SNOWY CHOCOLATE TRUFFLES

MAKES APPROXIMATELY 12-16

75g/3oz unsalted butter
100g/4oz icing sugar, sifted
225g/8oz white chocolate, very gently melted (see
page 41)
1 × 15ml spoon/1 tablespoon brandy
DECORATION
ground almonds or cocoa powder

Beat the butter and icing sugar together until creamy. Stir in the chocolate and brandy. Stir until thick and cooled. Chill until firm. Shape into walnut-sized balls. Roll in ground almonds or cocoa powder. Chill before packing in a rigid container, or a small basket for a pretty effect.

CARAMEL ALMOND TART

SERVES 6-8

PASTRY
175g/6oz plain flour, sifted
1 × 15ml spoon/1 tablespoon caster sugar
100g/4oz butter
3-4 × 5ml spoons/3-4 teaspoons water
FILLING
175g/6oz flaked almonds
175ml/6fl oz double cream
175g/6oz sugar
few drops almond essence
1 orange, finely grated rind
1 × 15ml spoon/1 tablespoon orange juice

To make the pastry, sift together the flour and sugar. Rub in the butter finely. Mix to a firm dough with the water. Wrap in polythene film and chill for 30 minutes. Roll out on a lightly floured work surface and use to line a 20cm/8inch flan tin. Chill again for 30 minutes. Bake the pastry 'blind' at 190°C/375°F/Gas 5 for 15 to 20 minutes.

To make the filling, place all the ingredients in a pan and bring to the boil. Turn down the heat and simmer very gently, stirring constantly, for 10 to 15 minutes until the sugar dissolves. Pour into the pastry case and bake for a further 20 to 25 minutes until set. Allow to cool and transport in the tin. Serve cut into slices.

STOLLEN

SERVES 8

450g/1 lb strong plain flour
1 × 5ml spoon/1 teaspoon salt
1 sachet easy-blend dried yeast
75g/3oz caster sugar
100g/4oz butter, melted
300ml/½ pint lukewarm milk
2 eggs, beaten
½ lemon, grated rind only
50g/2oz blanched almonds, chopped
75g/3oz glacé cherries, chopped
100g/4oz candied peel
175g/6oz sultanas
DECORATION
icing sugar

Sift the flour and salt into a large warmed bowl. Stir in the yeast and sugar. Blend the melted butter with the milk and eggs and pour into the flour. Mix to a dough and turn out onto a lightly floured surface. Knead for 10 minutes until the dough is soft and no longer sticky. Place in an oiled polythene bag and allow to rise in a warm place for 1 hour until doubled in size. Knock back the dough and knead in the remaining ingredients. Shape the dough into a large flat oval and fold one side over the other lengthways. Place on a greased baking sheet and cover with oiled polythene film. Leave to prove in a warm place for another hour. Remove the film and bake at 200°C/400°F/Gas 6 for about 45 minutes until the loaf is golden-brown and sounds hollow when tapped underneath. Allow to cool on a wire rack.

Dust with icing sugar and, for a festive look, tie with ribbons. Wrap in foil to transport and serve in slices.

VARIATION Make individual stollen by shaping the dough into rings or plaits, and tying a name to each baked cake with ribbon.

ST CLEMENT'S MERINGUE PIE

SERVES 4-6

100g/4oz shortcrust pastry
FILLING
75g/3oz caster sugar
300ml/½ pint water
1 lemon, grated rind and juice
1 orange, grated rind and juice
1 lime, grated rind and juice
50g/2oz cornflour
3 egg yolks
TOPPING
3 egg whites
175g/6oz caster sugar

Line a 20cm/8 inch fluted flan tin or dish with the pastry. Bake blind at 190°C/375°F/Gas 5 for 15 to 20 minutes. Allow to cool. To make the filling, dissolve the sugar in the water in a small pan. Add the grated rinds and boil for 5 minutes. Blend the cornflour with the fruit juices and pour the sugar syrup onto the cornflour mixture. Return to the pan and cook gently, stirring, until thickened. Remove from the heat and stir in the egg yolks. Spread the filling into the prepared pastry case.

To make the topping, whisk the egg whites until very stiff. Whisk in half the sugar then whisk again until stiff. Fold in the remaining sugar. Pipe or pile on top of the filling in the case. Bake at 180°C/350°F/Gas 4 for 30 minutes until the top is just coloured. Cool and transport in the tin or dish. Serve with cream.

HOT SPICED MULL

SERVES 6-8

3 × 5ml spoons/3 teaspoons caster sugar
1 bottle dry red wine
1 cinnamon stick
5 coriander seeds
6 cloves
½ orange, thinly pared rind
½ lemon, thinly pared rind
1 × 15ml spoon/1 tablespoon orange curaçao or
brandy

Mix the sugar, wine, cinnamon, coriander, cloves and citrus rind in a large pan. Heat gently until the sugar dissolves and the mixture is just below simmering point. Add the liqueur or brandy and pour into flasks.

To serve, strain into glasses.

VARIATION   *Cider Glow*
Make as for the Hot Spiced Mull but replace the wine with a bottle of dry, still cider. Use Calvados (apple brandy) instead of curaçao.

HONEY GLOGG

SERVES 8

50g/2oz seedless raisins
1 × 5ml spoon/1 teaspoon ground cloves
1 × 5ml spoon/1 teaspoon ground cinnamon
1 × 5ml spoon/1 teaspoon ground cardamom
6 × 15ml spoons/6 tablespoons clear honey
1 bottle dry red wine
150ml/¼ pint brandy

Place all the ingredients except the brandy in a large pan. Cover and heat very gently for about 1 hour to allow the flavours to mingle. Remove from the heat and pour in the brandy. Pour into flasks and serve in small cups.

SPRING EXCURSION

The first signs of spring herald the start of the summer picnic season, and what better way to celebrate than with a picnic of gargantuan proportions. The food should reflect the creative extravagance of the natural world – this is no time to be reticent.

Soup is still a welcome sight at this time of the year, and Tropical Lentil Soup is wholesome and exotic. Serve it with a variety of starters: Brandied Liver Pâté with crackers and celery; Bacon and Pinenut Filo Wheels; and Chillied Prawns with Avocado Cream. Warming casseroles can be transported to the picnic in wide-necked flasks; provide a choice so that guests can try a bit of each. Rich Beef and Beetroot Hotpot is served with Mushroom and Parsley Pilau while the Orchard Pork Casserole goes well with wholemeal rolls and butter. Puff Top Chicken and Walnut Pies are best eaten hot as an accompaniment, or alternative to the casseroles.

For a festive touch, present an Easter Braid Garland surrounded by Marbled Chocolate Eggs and a selection of desserts, to finish.

BRANDIED LIVER PÂTÉ

APPETIZER   SERVES 4-6

450g/1 lb chicken livers
¼ × 5ml spoon/¼ teaspoon salt
pinch nutmeg, freshly grated
pinch ground cloves
pinch ground cinnamon
½ × 5ml spoon/½ teaspoon dried mixed herbs
1 clove garlic, peeled and crushed
50ml/2 fl oz brandy
225g/8 oz butter
2 × 15ml spoons/2 tablespoons double cream
GARNISH
100g/4 oz unsalted butter, clarified (see page 78 for
method)

Trim any stringy membranes from the livers and place in a shallow dish with the salt, spices, herbs, garlic and brandy. Cover and leave to marinate for several hours. Melt the butter in a large heavy frying pan. Drain the livers and reserve the marinade juices. Add the livers to the butter and fry for 3 to 4 minutes, until firm but still pink in the centre. Remove the livers and place in a liquidiser or blender. Pour the marinade juices into the butter in the pan and cook for 2 minutes. Pour the contents of the pan over the livers and blend to a purée. Stir in the cream and pour the pâté into small pots. Chill until set. Finish with a layer of clarified butter on top of each pot to seal. Chill.

Transport in the pots and serve with crackers and celery.

BACON AND PINENUT FILO WHEELS

APPETIZER   MAKES 6-8

225g/8oz bacon, rinds removed and chopped
25g/1oz butter
1 onion, peeled and chopped
1 carrot, peeled and finely chopped
100g/4oz fresh breadcrumbs
100g/4oz pinenuts
2 × 15ml spoons/2 tablespoons fresh parsley,
chopped
1 egg, beaten
8 sheets filo pastry
75g/3oz melted butter

Fry the bacon in the butter for 1 minute. Add the vegetables and fry for 5 minutes until soft. Remove from the heat. Stir in the breadcrumbs, pinenuts and parsley. Season with freshly-ground black pepper. Bind together with the egg.

Have the sheets of pastry in a stack and fold in half to form a 'book'. Brush each sheet of pastry with melted butter, gently turning the 'pages' as you go. Lay the pastry pile open flat and spread the breadcrumb mixture over the top sheet, leaving 5cm/2inch clear at one short side. Roll up all 8 sheets together from the opposite side finishing with the join underneath. Chill the roll for 30 minutes.

Cut the roll into 2cm/¾ inch slices and place them on a baking sheet. Brush the slices with any remaining melted butter and bake at 190°C/375°F/ Gas 5 for 30 minutes. Cool on a wire rack.

Pack in a rigid container.

CHILLIED PRAWNS AND AVOCADO CREAM

APPETIZER   SERVES 4-6

350g/12oz large peeled prawns
MARINADE
2 × 15ml spoons/2 tablespoons olive oil
1 clove garlic, peeled and crushed
pinch chilli powder
1 × 5ml spoon/1 teaspoon soy sauce
few drops Tabasco sauce
freshly-ground black pepper
AVOCADO CREAM
1 avocado pear
2 × 15ml spoons/2 tablespoons lemon juice
75g/3oz curd cheese
½ red pepper, cored, deseeded and finely chopped

Thread the prawns, 3 together, onto wooden cocktail sticks. Blend together the oil, garlic, chilli, soy and Tabasco sauce and plenty of freshly-ground black pepper. Place the mixture in a large shallow container and add the skewered prawns. Chill and marinate for several hours.

To make the avocado cream, peel and stone the avocado pear and mash the flesh with the lemon juice and curd cheese until smooth. Stir in the red pepper and season to taste.

Pack the cream into a small sealed container and chill. Cover the marinade dish, with the prawns and marinade in it, and drain just before serving with the cream dip.

TROPICAL LENTIL SOUP

SERVES 6

100g/4oz split red lentils
2 × 15ml spoons/2 tablespoons oil
1 onion, peeled and chopped
2 carrots, peeled and chopped
2 sticks celery, trimmed and chopped
3 rashers streaky bacon, rinds removed, chopped
1 green pepper, cored, deseeded and chopped
1 × 5ml spoon/1 teaspoon wholegrain mustard
1 × 5ml spoons/1 teaspoon *garam marsala*
50g/2oz creamed coconut
900ml/1½ pints stock
1 × 15ml spoon/1 tablespoon tomato purée
freshly-ground black pepper
TO SERVE
fresh cream

Soak the lentils in boiling water for 10 minutes. Drain. Heat the oil in a large pan and fry the onion, carrot, celery, bacon and pepper for 5 minutes. Add the mustard, *garam marsala* and lentils and cook for 2 minutes. Stir in the coconut, stock and tomato purée. Season with freshly-ground black pepper. Bring to the boil, cover and simmer for 50 minutes. Purée the soup in a liquidiser or food processor until almost smooth.

Transport in a flask and serve hot with a little cream spooned on top.

MUSHROOM AND PARSLEY PILAU

MAIN DISH   SERVES 4-6

50g/2oz butter
1 bunch spring onions, trimmed and chopped
175g/6oz long grain rice or risotto rice
175g/6oz button mushrooms, sliced
freshly-ground black pepper
750ml/1¼ pints chicken stock
4 × 15ml spoons/4 tablespoons fresh parsley, chopped
25g/1oz Parmesan cheese, freshly grated
pinch freshly grated nutmeg

Melt the butter in a large shallow pan. Add the spring onions and rice and cook for 3 to 4 minutes without colouring. Stir in the mushrooms and stock and season with plenty of freshly-ground black pepper. Bring to the boil. Cover and simmer for about 30 minutes or until the rice is tender and the liquid is nearly absorbed. Stir in the parsley, cheese and nutmeg.

Place in a wide-necked flask for transporting, hot, to the picnic.

VARIATION   *Mushroom Rice Salad*
Make as for the Mushroom and Parsley Pilau. Allow the mixture to cool when cooked. Stir through 2 × 15ml spoons/2 tablespoons vinaigrette dressing before serving.

PUFF TOP CHICKEN AND WALNUT PIES

MAIN DISH   MAKES 6

2 × 15ml spoons/2 tablespoons oil
4 large chicken pieces
1 leek, trimmed and sliced
1 onion, peeled and sliced
300ml/½ pint chicken stock
25g/1 oz butter
1 × 15 ml spoon/1 tablespoon flour
150ml/¼ pint single cream
freshly-ground white pepper
75g/3 oz walnuts, broken into pieces
PASTRY
350g/12 oz plain flour
pinch salt
pinch mustard powder
75g/3 oz butter
75g/3 oz shortening
iced water to mix
225g/8 oz puff pastry
beaten egg, to glaze

Heat the oil in a flameproof casserole. Add the chicken pieces and fry briskly until browned on all sides. Add the leek and onion and fry for 1 minute. Pour in the stock and season. Cover and cook for 1 hour, simmering gently, until tender. Cool. Remove the skin and bones from the chicken. Tear the meat into small pieces and set aside with the strained vegetables. Reserve the stock.

Melt the butter in a small pan and add the flour. Cook for 2 minutes. Stir in 6 × 15ml spoons/ 6 tablespoons of the reserved chicken stock and blend in the cream. Beat until smooth and cook for 3 minutes. Season with freshly-ground white pepper. Cool. Stir in the chicken meat and vegetables and add the walnuts.

To make the pastry, sift the flour, salt and mustard into a bowl. Rub in the butter and shortening and stir in just enough iced water to mix to a firm dough. Roll out and use to line 6 ramekin dishes. Divide the creamed chicken filling between the pies.

Roll out the puff pastry and cut out 6 rounds to make lids for the pies. Dampen the edges of the pastry and press on the lids. From the remaining puff pastry cut out decorations and attach to the lids with beaten egg. Cut a slit in each to allow the steam to escape and brush all over with beaten egg. Place the pies on a baking sheet and bake at 220°C/425°F/Gas 7 for 15 minutes then reduce the heat to 190°C/375°F/Gas 5 for a further 15 minutes. Cover with foil if the tops begin to over-brown.

To eat hot at the picnic, pack the ramekins into a large biscuit tin lined with tea-towels. Wrap the tin in more towels and place in an insulated bag. Serve hot, removing the pies from the ramekins just before serving.

ORCHARD PORK CASSEROLE

MAIN DISH   SERVES 6-8

3 green-skinned dessert apples
1 red-skinned dessert apple
450 g/1 lb pears
1 lemon, grated rind and juice
900g/2 lb pork fillet, cubed
50g/2oz butter
2 onions, peeled and sliced
175g/6oz smoked pork sausage, sliced
600ml/1 pint stock
freshly-ground black pepper
1 × 15ml spoon/1 tablespoon fresh parsley, chopped
1 × 15ml spoon/1 tablespoon fresh sage, chopped

Peel, core and slice the fruit and toss in the lemon rind and juice. Fry the pork in the butter in a flameproof casserole until browned on all sides. Add the onions and fry for 3 minutes. Stir in the sausage and stock and season with freshly-ground black pepper. Cover and cook for 1 hour over very gentle heat. Add the herbs and fruit and continue to cook for another 40 minutes.

Transport in a wide-necked flask and serve hot with wholemeal rolls and butter.

RICH BEEF AND BEETROOT HOTPOT

MAIN DISH   SERVES 4-6

900g/2 lb braising steak
3 × 15ml spoons/3 tablespoons oil
1 large onion, peeled and sliced
3 sticks celery, sliced
350g/12oz flat mushrooms, sliced
2 × 5ml spoons/2 teaspoons fresh horseradish, grated
1 × 5ml spoon/1 teaspoon wholegrain mustard
freshly-ground black pepper
450g/1 lb raw beetroot, peeled and sliced
300ml/½ pint red wine or stock

Trim the beef and cut it into large cubes or strips. Heat the oil in a large flameproof casserole until it is very hot and fry the beef, in batches, to seal it. Remove the meat from the casserole. Fry the onion and celery for 3 minutes, then add the mushrooms and fry for a further 3 minutes. Return the meat to the casserole and stir in the horseradish, mustard and plenty of freshly-ground black pepper. Stir in the beetroot and red wine (or stock) and cover. Cook at 150°C/300°F/Gas 2 for 3 to 4 hours until very tender. Pour into a wide-necked food flask for transportation and seal. Serve hot with Mushroom and Parsley Pilau (page 108).

POTATO CHESTNUT CASSEROLE

MAIN DISH   SERVES 6

450g/1 lb fresh chestnuts
750g/1½ lb potatoes, peeled, cut into cubes
150ml/¼ pint milk
150ml/¼ pint double cream
pinch freshly grated nutmeg
salt, freshly-ground black pepper
25g/1 oz Gruyère cheese, grated

Make a deep slit in the skin of each chestnut. Place them in a roasting tin with a 300ml/½ pint water and bake at 200°C/400°F/Gas 6 for 10 to 15 minutes until the skins burst open. Allow to cool slightly. Remove the outer shells and the inner brown skin. Mix the potatoes and chestnuts in a casserole dish. Heat the milk and cream together to just below boiling point. Stir in the nutmeg, salt and freshly-ground black pepper. Pour over the potatoes and chestnuts and sprinkle with the cheese. Cover and cook in a 200°C/400°F/Gas 6 oven for 45 minutes. Remove the lid and cook for a further 15 minutes until the top has browned.

To transport and eat hot at the picnic, cover the casserole with the lid and wrap it in towels or a blanket, then put the whole parcel in an insulated bag.

Serve with the Puff Top Chicken and Walnut Pies (page 109).

PORK, APPLE AND JUNIPER PIE

SERVES 4-6

25g/1 oz butter
2 × 15ml spoons/2 tablespoons oil
750g/1½ lb pork tenderloin, trimmed and cubed
1 leek, trimmed and sliced
1 onion, sliced
8 juniper berries, crushed
2 × 15ml spoons/2 tablepoons tomato purée
300ml/½ pint stock
1 bouquet garni
3 dessert apples, peeled, cored and cubed
PASTRY
750/1½ lb plain flour
2 × 5ml spoons/2 teaspoons salt
100g/4 oz lard
50g/2 oz butter
300ml/½ pint water
1 egg, beaten
1 teaspoon gelatine

To make the filling, heat the butter and oil in a flameproof casserole dish. Fry the pork until browned on all sides. Add the leek and onion and fry for 5 minutes. Stir in the remaining ingredients except the apples. Simmer the casserole for 1 hour, add the apples and cook for a further 20 minutes. Drain off the stock and reserve. Cool the filling.

To make the pastry, sift the flour and salt into a large mixing bowl. Make a well in the centre. Place the lard, butter and water in a small pan. Heat until melted then bring to the boil. Pour into the flour and quickly mix to a fairly soft dough. Turn out onto a lightly floured surface and knead until smooth. Reserve one quarter of the pastry. Use the remaining pastry to line the base and sides of a large raised pie mould or cake tin.

Spoon the prepared filling into the case and level the top. Roll out the reserved pastry and use to cover the pie and make a lid. Dampen the edges of the crusts to seal. Trim, crimp the crusts and decorate with the trimmings. Make a 12mm/½ inch hole in the centre of the lid. Brush the top of the pie with beaten egg and bake at 200°C/400°F/Gas 6 for 30 minutes. Brush again with beaten egg and reduce the oven temperature to 170°C/325°F/Gas 3 for 45 minutes until golden-brown. Dissolve the gelatine in the reserved stock and as the pie cools, pour it through the hole in the lid. Chill overnight. Transport in the tin and turn out before serving.

COFFEE CHOUX PUFFS

MAKES 10-12

50g/2oz butter
150ml/¼ pint water
65g/2½oz strong plain flour
2 eggs, beaten
FILLING
300ml/½ pint double cream
few drops vanilla essence
2 × 15ml spoons/2 tablespoons caster sugar
ICING
100g/4oz icing sugar
1 × 5ml spoon/1 teaspoon coffee essence
2 × 15ml spoons/2 tablespoons nibbed almonds

Place the butter and water in a small pan. Heat gently until the butter melts and bring to the boil. Add the flour all at once and beat, over the heat for 2 minutes until the mixture comes away from the sides of the pan. Allow to cool slightly. Gradually beat in the egg, adding just enough to give a fairly stiff, smooth glossy paste. Place in a large piping bag fitted with a plain nozzle and pipe rounds the size of ping-pong balls onto greased baking sheets. Bake at 220°C/425°F/Gas 7 for 20 to 25 minutes until very crisp and light. Cool on a wire rack.

To make the filling, whip the cream, vanilla and sugar until it stands in peaks. Split the puffs and fill them with the cream.

To make the icing, blend the icing sugar with the coffee essence and just enough water to make a thick glaze. Spread a little icing over each puff. Allow to dry before packing in a rigid container. Chill before transporting.

HALVA YOGHURT

SERVES 4-6

3 large cooking apples, peeled, cored and chopped
1 × 15ml spoon/1 tablespoon lemon juice
1 × 15ml spoon/1 tablespoon caster sugar
25g/1oz butter
600ml/1 pint thick Greek yoghurt
100g/4oz pistachio, almond or vanilla halva (ready-made), chopped
DECORATION
Fresh mint sprigs

Place the apples, lemon juice, sugar and butter in a pan. Stir in 1 × 15ml spoon/1 tablespoon water and cover the pan tightly. Cook very gently for about 10 minutes, shaking the pan frequently until the apples are reduced to a thick pulp. Cool. Stir the apple into the yoghurt and finally stir in the halva. Chill and pack into individual sealed containers or a wide-necked food flask.

DRIED FRUIT COMPOTE

SERVES 6-8

100g/4 oz each of dried pears, peaches, apple rings,
papaya, pineapple, figs and apricots or any preferred
combination
1.1 litres/2 pints strong hot tea
100g/4 oz demerara sugar
1 × 5ml spoon/1 teaspoon ground cinnamon
4 × 15ml spoons/4 tablespoons rum
100g/4 oz stoned dates

Mix the dried fruit in a large bowl. Dissolve the
sugar in the tea and add the cinnamon and rum.
Pour the mixture over the fruit and leave to stand
overnight. Pour into a sealed container and stir in
the dates. Chill before packing. Serve with whipped cream or thick Greek yoghurt.

SPRING SPECIAL

SERVES 6

600ml/1 pint fresh orange juice
2 × 15ml spoons/2 tablespoons grenadine syrup
100ml/4 fl oz Tia Maria liqueur
TO SERVE
600ml/1 pint sparkling mineral water
fresh mint sprigs

Mix the orange juice, grenadine and liqueur in a
chilled flask. Just before serving mix in the mineral
water and float mint sprigs on the surface.

FROSTED CHOCOLATE GÂTEAU

SERVES 8-10

SPONGE ROLL
3 eggs
75g/3oz caster sugar
75g/3oz plain flour, sifted
FILLING
225g/8oz plain chocolate, grated
300ml/½ pint double cream
1 × 15ml spoon/1 tablespoon dark rum
FROSTING
225g/8oz caster sugar
4 × 15ml spoons/4 tablespoons water
pinch cream of tartar
1 egg white

To make the sponge roll, whisk the eggs and sugar together until very thick, pale and fluffy. Gently fold in the flour and pour the mixture into a greased, lined 23 × 33cm/9 × 13inch swiss roll tin. Bake at 200°C/400°F/Gas 6 for 12 to 15 minutes. Turn out onto sugared greaseproof paper. Peel off the lining paper and trim the edges. Roll up the sponge with the paper inside. Cool on a wire rack.

To make the filling, place the chocolate, cream and rum in a pan over a gentle heat and stir until blended. Bring briefly to the boil and immediately remove from the heat. Allow to cool until thickened, stirring occasionally. Whisk the mixture until thick and fluffy. Unroll the sponge, spread with the filling and re-roll.

To make the frosting, place the sugar and water in a small pan and heat gently, stirring, until the sugar dissolves. Add the cream of tartar and bring to the boil. Without stirring, boil until the temperature reaches 118°C/240°F on a sugar thermometer (soft ball stage). Meanwhile whisk the egg white until stiff. As soon as the syrup has reached the correct temperature remove from the heat and when the bubbles have subsided, pour the syrup in a thin stream on to the egg white while continuing to whisk. Whisk the mixture until it is very thick (about 3 minutes). Quickly swirl the frosting over the roll. Allow to set.

Pack in a rigid container and serve in slices.

MARBLED CHOCOLATE EGGS

MAKES 6-8

350g/12oz good quality plain cooking chocolate
175g/6oz white chocolate

Grate the chocolate into separate jugs. Stand each jug in a bowl of hot water and stir until the chocolate melts. The chocolate should be at 35°C/94°F when ready to use. Polish the inside of small egg-shaped chocolate moulds with cotton wool. Pour the melted chocolates into a large bowl and stir them together briefly. Pour the chocolate into the moulds to fill and leave them in a cool dry place until the outside layer of chocolate has set to a leathery consistency. Pour or spoon the remaining liquid chocolate out of the egg moulds. Trim the edges of the eggs with a knife to make a smooth finish. Allow to stand until completely set.

Gently tap the moulds on a surface to release the shapes. Turn out the egg halves. Sandwich the egg halves together in pairs using a little melted chocolate. Pack in a padded container and keep cool.

TO DECORATE The eggs can be decorated with piped lines and loops of icing, or small crystallised fruits or flowers.

POPPYSEED DIGESTIVE BISCUITS

MAKES 25

175g/6oz wholemeal flour
100g/4oz medium oatmeal
¼ × 5ml spoon/¼ teaspoon salt
pinch of dry mustard
75g/3oz butter
4 × 15ml spoons/4 tablespoons milk
1 egg, beaten
2-3 × 15ml spoons/2-3 tablespoons poppy seeds

Mix the flour, oatmeal, salt and dry mustard in a bowl. Rub in the butter. Stir in the milk and half the egg and mix to a firm dough. Knead lightly and roll out thinly on a lightly floured surface. Cut out 7.5cm/3inch rounds with a biscuit cutter. Place on greased baking sheets. Brush with the remaining egg and sprinkle with the poppyseeds. Bake at 200°C/400°F/Gas 6 for 12 to 15 minutes until golden. Cool on a wire rack.

Transport in polythene bags.

WALNUT BREAD

MAKES 2 SMALL LOAVES

15g/½oz fresh yeast
300ml/½ pint hand-hot water
450g/1 lb wholemeal flour
1½ × 5ml spoons/1½ teaspoons salt
15g/½ oz butter
3 spring onions, trimmed and chopped
50g/2oz walnuts, chopped
beaten egg, to glaze
sesame seeds

Blend the yeast and water together. Mix the flour and salt in a warmed bowl. Rub in the butter and stir in the onions and nuts. Pour in the yeast liquid and mix to a soft dough.

Turn out onto a lightly floured surface and knead until soft and smooth for about 10 minutes. Cut the dough in half and shape each into a roll. Place each in a small greased loaf tin and cover with oiled polythene film. Leave to rise in a warm place for about 1 hour until doubled in size. Remove the film, brush with beaten egg and sprinkle with seeds. Bake at 230°C/450°F/Gas 8 for 25 minutes until golden-brown and the rolls sound hollow when tapped underneath. Cool on a wire rack.

EASTER BRAID GARLAND

SERVES 8

15g/½oz fresh yeast
150ml/¼ pint lukewarm milk
225g/8oz strong plain flour
½ × 5ml spoon/½ teaspoon salt
2 × 5ml spoons/2 teaspoons sugar
25g/1oz butter
FILLING
25g/1oz butter, melted
25g/1oz walnuts, coarsely chopped
25g/1oz glacé cherries, quartered
75g/3oz dried apricots, chopped
25g/1oz sultanas
50g/2oz soft brown sugar
DECORATION
icing sugar for glaze

Blend the yeast with the milk. Sift the flour and salt into a large warmed bowl. Stir in the sugar and rub in the butter. Pour in the yeast liquid and mix to a soft dough. Turn out on to a floured surface and knead until smooth and silky. Place in an oiled polythene bag and leave to rise in a warm place until doubled in size. Knock back the risen dough and knead until smooth again. Roll out on a lightly floured surface to a large rectangle. Brush the dough with the melted butter and scatter the nuts, fruit and sugar over the surface. Roll up the dough from a long side like a swiss roll.

With a sharp knife, cut the roll in half lengthways to make 2 long half-rolls. Press the strips together at one end and then twist them together. Form the twisted dough into a ring and set on a greased baking sheet. Cover with oiled polythene film and leave to prove in a warm place for about 20 minutes until puffy.

Remove the film and bake the garland at 220°C/425°F/Gas 7 for about 40 minutes until golden-brown. While still hot mix a little sifted icing sugar with enough boiling water to form a thin cream. Brush this glaze over the garland and allow to cool on a wire rack. When cold, wind a ribbon round the garland and tie in a bow to decorate.

Serve in slices.

HOT CROSS BUNS

MAKES 16

25g/1oz fresh yeast
300ml/½ pint hand-hot milk
450g/1lb strong plain flour
1 × 5ml spoon/1 teaspoon salt
2 × 15ml spoons/2 tablespoons caster sugar
50g/2oz butter
1½ × 5ml spoon/1½ teaspoons ground mixed spice
100g/4oz currants
50g/2oz mixed peel
DECORATION
75g/3oz plain flour
2 × 15ml spoons/2 tablespoons oil
water
GLAZE
50g/2oz caster sugar
5 × 15ml spoons/5 tablespoons milk

Blend the yeast with the water. Sift the flour into a bowl with the salt and sugar. Rub in the butter and stir in the spice. Pour in the yeast liquid and mix to a soft dough. Turn out onto a lightly floured work surface and knead until soft, smooth and silky. Place in an oiled polythene bag and leave to rise in a warm place until doubled in size. Knock back the dough and knead in the fruit and peel. Divide the dough into about 16 pieces and roll each into a ball. Place, well-spaced, on greased baking sheets and cover with oiled polythene film. Allow to prove in a warm place for about 40 minutes.

For the decoration, blend the flour and oil and add just enough water to make a dough slack enough for piping. Spoon into a paper piping bag and snip off the end. Remove the film from the buns and pipe crosses of the mixture over each. Bake at 220°C/425°F/Gas 7 for 15 to 20 minutes until golden-brown.

Meanwhile, place the sugar and milk for the glaze in a small pan. Bring to the boil and simmer for 4 minutes. Brush this glaze over the buns as they come out of the oven. Cool on a wire rack.

Serve split and buttered.

PERFECT PICNIC TIPS

Even spur-of-the-moment family outings can be turned into perfect picnics. Ready-made vol-au-vent cases can be used with quickly made fillings such as taramasalata, blue cheese and dressed crab beaten to a smooth mixture with cream cheese and seasonings. Or spread celery sticks with a filling, or serve sticks of celery, carrot and cucumber with cups of filling for a dip. Buy croissants, split and fill them with cheese, ham and tomatoes. Sandwich ratafia biscuits together with a little vanilla butter cream for a quick 'dessert'. Spread icing on the top of Madeira cake and cut the cake into squares. Top each square with a crystallised violet or rose petal.

KEEPING FOOD HOT
Soups, casseroles and stews can be kept hot in wide-necked food flasks. For a larger quantity, seal and then wrap a casserole in thick towels or blankets and put the whole into an insulated bag. Alternatively, set the hot container into a large cardboard box filled with straw, cover with straw, then seal the box lid. Keep pasties hot in the same way, packed in a biscuit tin lined with kitchen paper to absorb the steam. If there is to be a long period before the food is eaten, it may be more effective to take a small camping stove and reheat the food on arrival.

If you are picnicking on a hike or ramble, take very lightweight containers for the food so that they can be carried without discomfort after the meal. Pack squashable foods into foil parcels or use polythene bags. Small, sealable plastic tubs and beakers are ideal, light-weight containers. Choose those that fit inside each other when empty so that they take up less space.

Christmas left-overs make excellent picnic foods and this is an ideal way of using up pieces of cooked turkey, ham and beef. Mix cooked meats with raw sliced mushrooms and spiced mayonnaise and serve in pitta bread pockets. Spread slices of cooked beef with wholegrain mustard or creamed horseradish and roll up to eat with crusty french bread. Christmas cake and mince pies are good for impromptu picnics – warm the pies and pack them in a biscuit tin lined with absorbent kitchen paper.

DRINKS
Plenty of drinks are essential for a perfect picnic, cool and long for summer, steaming hot for cold weather. Tea and coffee are best freshly made on site from a flask of boiling water or better still, a kettle on a small camping burner. For cold drinks, crushed ice in insulated flasks or jugs will help. In very hot weather, freeze the drink completely and it will be ready to drink ice-cold, by the time it is served. Very sweet drinks tend to increase thirst and are better avoided.

Look for unbreakable bottles in plastic or aluminium. Check that the stoppers, lids or seals really do work – even upside down. You don't want a knapsack awash with orange squash! Insulated flasks are ideal for hot drinks – look for those with non-breakable inners. Insulated jugs look good but are only suitable for a picnic with transport, as are the large pump-action flasks. These save you having to lift the flask to pour but they are cumbersome.

CHILDREN'S PICNICS
Children love to see their names written on food. Pipe names or initials in royal icing on fairy cakes, jellies and biscuits. Use pastry or cookie cutters to stamp initials in sandwiches. Smaller children will especially enjoy an individual party picnic hamper. Provide each child with a small box containing a selection of party foods. Tie the box with ribbon and attach a name label.

INSECTS AND SAND
Picnics on summer evenings, whether in the countryside or in the garden can be spoiled by flying insects. Light the area with barbecue garden flares, gas lanterns or candles set in glass covers or in jars on poles. Take the precaution of using a special slow-burning light designed to keep mosquitos at bay, especially near water.

Picnicking on a dry, wind-blown beach can be spoiled if sand is allowed to encroach on the food. Pack foods in lidded containers with deep sides, so that they do not fall over. Set the picnic out on a large clean cloth or towel. Take face towels dipped into cologne-scented water and packed in plastic bags to clean sticky, salty hands and faces. Provide plenty of soft paper napkins.

COOLING IT

There is almost nothing worse to eat than a warm tuna mousse and its a good idea to try and keep picnic foods chilled. A variety of insulated carry boxes are available; some are rigid with fitted lids while others are made of flexible padded plastic with zip closures. The latter have the advantage of folding smaller when empty. Ice packs will help keep the container's inside temperature down and food will stay chilled for several hours.

For an elegant occasion, pack a bag of ice cubes into a wine cooler, and cool the wine thoroughly before leaving home. Wrap the cooled bottles, and put them into the ice cooler immediately you arrive at the picnic site.

WATER COOLER

On a hot day, water can act as a perfect 'refrigerator' for bottled and canned drinks. Stand them securely between rocks in a fast flowing stream or bury them in wet sand at the shore line. Be sure to keep an eye on them though – especially when the tide comes in! At the lake-side, tie unopened bottles and cans into a string bag, submerge it in the water and secure the handles to the bank. When a cool drink is demanded – just haul them in!

GOOD PRESENTATION

For an elegant picnic, there's nothing nicer than china plates, metal cutlery, real napery and glassware for wines and soft drinks. All of these can weigh heavily and need to be very carefully packed. As an alternative, non-breakable rigid plasticware is available in a variety of patterns and styles, and can also be used for garden entertaining or barbecues. Acrylic tumblers and goblets are lightweight and look and handle almost as well as glass.

CHECK LIST

To ensure a perfect picnic, make a check list of essential items so that nothing is left behind. Don't forget things such as corkscrews, bottle and can openers, a carving knife, salt, pepper and mustard, salad dressings and butter and sharp knives for cutting cheese, slicing cakes and peeling fruit. When packing, plates, cups and cutlery go in first, then the tablecloth and the rug on top. Then, everything comes out in the right order to spread the picnic.

PLANNING AHEAD FOR PICNICS

Pre-cooking and freezing will ensure that delicious snacks and sandwiches are readily to hand for spur-of-the-moment excursions, and special dishes for more formal picnics can be planned.

Most foods freeze well but there are a few items which should be avoided.

FOODS UNSUITABLE FOR FREEZING
- Hard-boiled eggs (including eggs in pies, sandwiches, etc. and Scotch eggs)
- Custards (including tarts)
- Soft meringue topping on desserts
- Mayonnaise-type salad dressings
- Milk puddings
- Royal icing on cakes or biscuits
- Salad vegetables
- Stuffed poultry, stuffings
- Foods with a high proportion of gelatine

CHOOSING PACKAGING
Whenever possible, cook foods in containers which can go directly into the freezer. Foods which will need reheating such as casseroles, soups and stews, can be frozen in rigid containers then transferred to ordinary cooking ware for reheating.

Large items, such as whole hams, salmon, terrines, etc. can be wrapped in foil or heavy polythene sheeting.

GENERAL GUIDELINES

GALANTINES, MEATLOAF, ETC. Prepare and cook in loaf tins lined with foil. Freeze in the tin, remove tin from foil for storage.
High Quality Storage Life   2 months
To use, thaw quickly.
Alternatively, freeze in slices with cling film separators. Pack in polythene for freezing.

CRAB AND LOBSTER   Cook fresh fish, cool and leave in shell. Wrap in heavy gauge polythene or foil.

Alternatively, remove fish from shell, pack into containers, cover and overwrap in polythene or foil.

High Quality Storage Life   1 month

To use, thaw 6-8 hours in the refrigerator.

SOUPS   Thicken soups with cornflour rather than flour when preparing. Seasoning may cause off-flavours, so season after thawing.

Freeze in rigid containers, leaving head space.

High Quality Storage Life   2 months

To use, reheat gently. (Rice, cheese, cream, etc. should be added after heating.)

PASTA DISHES WITH SAUCES   Prepare in a freezer dish, cool, cover and freeze.

High Quality Storage Life   2 months

To use, remove the cover, re-cover with foil and heat slowly in the oven.

MOUSSE   Prepare and set in freezer container. Cover, then freeze.

High Quality Storage Life   1 month

To use, thaw in the refrigerator for 3-4 hours.

SHORTCRUST PASTRY TARTS AND QUICHES
Pastry cases can be frozen raw, or baked and unfilled. For ready-filled cases, prepare and bake as usual, cool, remove from tin and open-freeze. Wrap in foil or polythene, store in a rigid box.

High Quality Storage Life   1 month

To use, thaw at room temperature 3 hours or unwrap and heat in a medium oven for 20 minutes.

CASSEROLES   Prepare and cook the dish, transfer to a freezer dish. Cool, cover and freeze.

High Quality Storage Life   2 months

To use, part-thaw, then transfer to an ovenware container. Cover and heat gently for 45 minutes or reheat from frozen in a double saucepan.

PÂTÉ   Prepare in foil containers, cool and cover, freeze.

High Quality Storage Life   1 month

To use, thaw in refrigerator 3 hours.

PERFECT PICNIC MENUS

The menus here are planned to serve parties of varying numbers and the recipes can usually be found within the chapter indicated.

Recipes are not given for foods and accompaniments without page references. These are suggestions to complement the menus.

AT THE WATER'S EDGE

MENU 1   SERVES 6-8

Poached Salmon   page 12
Avocado Swirl   page 11
Mushroom Terrine   page 11
New Potato Salad   page 16
(served with mixed green salad, brown rolls, butter)
Brown Bread Ice Cream   page 17
Brandy Snap Curls   page 17

MENU 2   SERVES 6-8

Chicken Cashew Salad   page 14
Filo Onion Tarts   page 10
Seafood Pasta Salad   page 14
(served with mixed salad, brown rolls, butter)
Rich Chocolate Slice   page 18
(Fromage Frais and cream with fresh
raspberries)
To drink: Summer Sparkler   page 19

MENU 3   SERVES 6-8

Mushroom Terrine   page 11
Orange Glazed Gammon   page 13
Sweet and Sour Carrot Salad   page 15
German Potato Salad   page 15
(served with a tomato and spring onion salad)
Creamy Pear and Walnut Flan   page 18
Brandy Snap Curls   page 17

MENU 4   SERVES 6-8

Filo Onion Tarts   page 10
Roast Pistachio Chicken   page 13
Omelette Salad   page 16
(served with a green salad and bread sticks)
Fragrant Honey Mousse   page 19
Rich Chocolate Slice   page 18
(a selection of seasonal fruit)

A WALK IN THE COUNTRY

MENU 1   SERVES 6

Pork and Cranberry Samosas   page 23
Garlic Tortilla Omelette in Pitta Bread   page 26
Vegetable Sticks and Blue Cheese Dip   page 24
Apple and Almond Danish Pastries   page 29
Choc Nut Rocks   page 30
To drink: Homemade Lemonade   page 31
(fresh fruit)

MENU 2   SERVES 6

Peppery Chicken Parcels   page 27
Spiced Meat Balls and Dip   page 26
Potted Stilton and crackers   page 22
(plus a coleslaw salad)
Gingered Almond Loaf   page 29
Apricot Brandy Cream Mousse   page 28

MENU 3   SERVES 6

Hearty Bean Soup   page 25
Sagey Pork Parcels   page 23
Taramasalata and Pitta bread   page 22
Creamy Mushroom Puffs   page 23
Apricot and Walnut Slice   page 29
Flaky Cheese and Apple Strudel   page 28

MENU 4   SERVES 6

Potted Danish Blue   page 22
Chicken and Veal Terrine   page 25
(wholemeal rolls and butter)
Fresh Tomato Chutney   page 24
Fruited Flapjack   page 30
Apple and Almond Danish Pastries   page 29

SUMMER INTERLUDE

MENU 1   SERVES 6-8

Prawn and Asparagus Mousse   page 35
(served with a celery and corn salad)
Mushroom Tart   page 35
Creamy Apple and Horseradish Chicken
page 37
Mixed Wild Rice Salad   page 38
Rosemary Bread Sticks   page 42
Japonaise Fingers   page 43
Kiwi Citrus Fruit Salad and cream   Page 40

MENU 2   SERVES 6-8

Raised Chicken and Ham Pie   page 37
Tricolour Vegetable Terrine   page 34
Greek Salad   page 39
Saffron Bread   page 42
Cassata   page 40
Florentines   page 43
(a selection of seasonal fresh fruit)

MENU 3   SERVES 6

Mozzarella and Tomato Salad   page 39
Rosemary Bread Sticks   page 42
Salad Niçoise   page 38
Salmon and Lemon Terrine   page 36
(serve with crusty bread, new potatoes, coleslaw and
a salad)
Poached Pears   page 41
Florentines   page 43
(a selection of cheeses)

MENU 4   SERVES 6

Seafood Cocktails   page 34
Olive and Anchovy Bread   page 42
Mixed Wild Rice Salad   page 38
(plus a coleslaw and a green salad)
Dark and White Chocolate Mousse   page 41
Japonaise Cakes   page 43

CHILDREN'S PICNICS

For birthday picnics, each menu to be supplemented
by a birthday cake of your choice

MENU 1   SERVES 8-10

Barbecue Chicken Chunks   page 46
Cheesy Snack Biscuits   page 46
Sesame Puff Fingers   page 49
Egg and Watercress Mini Loaves   page 50
(crisps, savoury nibbles)
Strawberry Cup Cakes   page 52
Lemon Meringue Ice Cream   page 54
To drink: fizzy bottled drinks or fruit juice

MENU 2   SERVES 8-10

Sausage Twirls   page 47
Buttered Cheese Bagels   page 47
Savoury Tomato Butterflies   page 48
Eggy Footballs   page 48
Caramel Fingers   page 53
Lime and Strawberry Jelly Mousse   page 53

MENU 3   SERVES 8-10

Egg and Watercress Mini Loaves   page 50
Cheese, Fruit and Nut Nibbles   page 50
Cheese and Celery Nut Bread   page 51
Mini Bacon Tarts   page 49
(crisps, celery and carrot sticks)
Chocolate Boxes   page 52

MENU 4   SERVES 8-10

Buttered Cheese Bagels   page 47
Barbecue Chicken Chunks   page 46
Herby Sausages with Mustard Dip   page 51
(crisps, savoury nibbles)
Lemon Cup Cakes   page 52
Caramel Fingers   page 53
Fresh Lemon and Lime Squash   page 54

FOOD FOR LOVE

MENU 1   SERVES 2

Spicy Potted Shrimps   page 58
Herbed French Stick with Garlic Butter
page 65
Tortellini and Sour Cream Salad   page 73
Watercress and Palm Heart Salad   page 74
Fondant Dipped Fruits   page 63
Orange and Rosewater Bavarois   page 62

MENU 2   SERVES 2

Blue Cheese, Bacon and Apple Salad   page 74
(wholemeal pitta bread)
Pork Satay   page 68
(Cucumber salad)
Chicken Tikka Pieces   page 60
Crab and Chicken Roll   page 60
Creamy Dutch Syllabub   page 64
Sponge Drops   page 63
(a selection of fresh fruit)

MENU 1   SERVES 8-10

Celery, Ham and Carrot Salad   page 72
Chicken Galantine   page 71
Cold Parslied Ratatouille Salad   page 72
Herbed French Stick with butter   page 65 (make
recipe × 3)
Cœur a la Creme   page 75
Fondant Dipped Fruits   page 63 (make recipe
× 4)

MENU 2   SERVES 6

Pork Satay   page 68 (make recipe × 3)
Savoury Stilton Milles Feuilles   page 69
Tortellini and Sour Cream Salad   page 73
Mushroom Brioches   page 67
(green salad)
Special Summer Pudding   page 75
Sponge Fingers   page 63 (make recipe × 3)
(a selection of cheeses)

AUTUMN BOUNTY

MENU 1   SERVES 8-10

Creamy Ham Croustades   page 79
Smoked Trout Baklava   page 78
Almond-filled Meringues   page 85
Crunchy Caramel Cones   page 86
Open Cherry Pies   page 84
Coffee Brazil Snaps   page 84

MENU 2   SERVES 8-10

Ham and Cheese Croissants   page 79
Ricotta and Smoked Salmon Parcels   page 81
Vegetable Crudités with Garlic and Walnut
Dip   page 80
(brown bread and butter)
Frangipane Tart   page 82
Sultana Streusel Cake   page 87
Paris Brest Gâteau   page 85

MENU 3   SERVES 6-8

Potted Tongue and crackers   page 78
Cheese and Mustard Cups   page 79
Vegetable Crudités with Green Herb Dip   page 80
Baked Plum Cheesecake   page 87
Raspberry Tartlets   page 84
To drink: Creamed Chocolate Drink   page 88

MENU 4   SERVES 6-8

Pinenut Savoury Bread   page 83
Veal and Tongue Terrine   page 80
(watercress and celery)
Honey and Sultana Drop Scones   page 82
Rose Petal Jelly   page 88
(bread and butter)
Chocolate Croissants   page 79
Paris Brest Gâteau   page 85

WINTER PICNICS

MENU 1   SERVES 6-8

Tomato Chowder   page 93
(wholemeal rolls and butter)
Mustardy Ham in Pastry   page 94
Peppered Roast Beef   page 96
Pink Grapefruit and Avocado Salad   page 98
(serve with mixed salad and mixed pickles)
Stollen   page 101
Orange and Almond Mince Pies with
Cointreau Butter   page 99

MENU 2   SERVES 6-8

Pink Grapefruit and Avocado Salad   page 98
Cassoulet Pot   page 92
(baked jacket potatoes)
French Beans Vinaigrette   page 98
Rum Babas   page 100
Snowy Chocolate Truffles   page 100
To drink: Hot Spiced Mull   page 102

MENU 3   SERVES 6-8

Chicken Noodle Soup   page 93
Beef Pastry Parcels   page 96
(serve with a mixed salad and a coleslaw salad)
Caramel Almond Tart   page 101
Stollen   page 101
To drink: Honey Glogg   page 102

MENU 4   SERVES 6-8

Creamy Pesto Tagliatelle Salad   page 97
Nutty Bacon Plait   page 95
French Beans Vinaigrette   page 98
Cocktail Tandoori Chicken   page 95
(celery and a cream, or blue-veined, cheese)
Orange and Almond Mince Pies and Brandied
Cream   page 99
To drink: Cider Glow   page 102

SPRING EXCURSION

MENU 1   SERVES 4-6

Brandied Liver Pâté   page 106
Poppyseed Digestive Biscuits   page 115
(served with celery)
Rich Beef and Beetroot Hotpot   page 110
Mushroom and Parsley Pilau   page 108
Easter Braid Garland   page 116
Marbled Chocolate Eggs   page 114

MENU 2   SERVES 4-6

Chillied Prawns and Avocado Cream   page 107
Puff Top Chicken and Walnut Pies   page 109
Potato Chestnut Casserole   page 111
(French stick and butter)
Halva Yogurt   page 112
Frosted Chocolate Gâteau   page 114
(served with whipped cream)
To drink: Spring Special   page 113

MENU 3   SERVES 4-6

Tropical Lentil Soup   page 108
Orchard Pork Casserole   page 110
Mushroom Rice Salad   page 108
Coffee Choux Puffs   page 112
Hot Cross Buns   page 116
Poppyseed Digestive Biscuits   page 115
(a selection of cheeses)

MENU 4   SERVES 6-8

Brandied Liver Pâté   page 106
(served with celery sticks)
Walnut Bread   page 115
Chillied Prawns and Avocado Cream   page 107
Bacon and Pinenut Filo Wheels   page 107
(serve with a mixed salad and a coleslaw salad)
Dried Fruit Compote   page 113
Halva Yogurt   page 112
To drink: Spring Special   page 113

INDEX